Innocence ***BEFORE*** Deception

By: Valarie D. Gray

(Formerly Thompson, the Daughter of a Pastor)

Purpose Publishing
1503 Main Street #168 • Grandview, Missouri
www.purposepublishing.com

ISBN: 978-0990301059

Editing by Felicia Murrell
Book Cover Design by PP Team of Designers

For permission and requests, write to the publisher:
1503 Main Street, #168, Grandview, MO 64030.

Author Inquiries may be sent to contactus@purposepublishing.com

Innocence BEFORE Deception takes you on a journey into the life of a young girl growing up in a simple and humble home. At age 15, naïve Valarie wanted to make friends at church, school and in the neighborhood. Like most teenage girls, she desired to have fun outside of her normal surroundings.

She never imagined such a deceptive plan crafted at the hands of others would take her innocence and force her to replay a tragic event affecting her life forever. Like many young victims, Valarie struggled to make sense of the horror she suffered. Although she chose to remain silent about the crime, her inner strength was remarkable as she trusted God to the very end.

Valarie shares her story in the hope of encouraging hearts to have compassion for young girls and women who navigate life feeling confused, isolated, and socially unsophisticated while enduring some of the most unimaginable life lessons as she depicts in, **Innocence BEFORE Deception.**

My Dedications

Dedicated to the memory of my son, Jaretton Jamal "JJ" Thompson, and two of my favorite aunts, Elyne Langrum and Caroline Yeldell, whom I LOVE and miss dearly.

God bless all the young girls and women living **through** private and public life events caused by the hands of others with the intention to break you down. You **SURVIVED** to live **YOUR** life, move forward!

My Special Acknowledgements

God is awesome! I know that without God my life would not be in a place of such peace. JJ is my number one fan, greatest inspiration and why I share our story. I thank JJ in my heart daily for helping me become the person I am today -- strong and humble.

Writing this message means I am finally walking in obedience to HIS will. Growing up in a ministry household I inherited LOTS of **ministry relatives**. In 2010, a ministry aunt prophesied that God wanted me to share my story, stating God would prepare me to be in the presence of people, especially women, because of my life journey in **Innocence BEFORE Deception**.

Thank you to ALL of the supportive people in my life. Thank you to two ministry aunts, Dr. Saundra Montgomery and Veda Shaw, special ladies Shree Moffett and Regina Nippert. You all stepped away from your busy lives to read my "terrible" rough draft and to offer me "real talk" to help start this process. For that, I am grateful. To two of my many sister-friends, Andrea White aka Dre and Irish Watson aka Yvette, neither of you stopped lending me your ears, eyes, hearts and hard criticism to finalize this project. Thank you.

To my kindhearted parents, Tommy Lee & Gloria Dunn Thompson, I LOVE you dearly. You did your best as I went through a very rough season of life. To my siblings, Michael, Carla, Lynda & Sheila, I LOVE you guys. We were young, however, you all cared enough to help a shy, shameful, naïve sister make it through. To Jarmelle, my only living child, God placed you in my life at the right time. I LOVE you son!

Most of us understand that nothing in life happens by chance. Derrice Gray, you are the man who asked me to be your "goofy" wife and I am forever honored.

A guy name Gregory aka "Pop" gave me a peace of mind at age sixteen and happens to be my husband's brother. Rest in peace my friend -- you did well by me. I will remember your every heartbeat, Jaretton Jamal Thompson, my first born. May you rest in peace until we meet again. I LOVE you JJ.

Table of Contents

1

The Bus Ride *To* Downtown Dallas

The grand event was finally here. The opening of the very popular State Fair of Texas located in South Dallas. Everyone's excitement surrounding the annually scheduled occasion was palpable, especially mine. Throughout the city there were all types of signs advertising the event. The city kicked off the grand opening of the fair with a full parade featuring local high school bands and large decorative floats. For as long as I could remember, everyone anticipated opening day.

The fair remained open for several weeks. Almost everyone I knew went. The school districts assigned us our very own day to attend. Special bus passes and free fair tickets were distributed to all the children. I accepted the pass and ticket every year, but I always gave my bus pass away because ever since I was a little girl, my parents drove us to the fair.

Fall, October 1981, was different. I was fifteen years old and my parents agreed to allow me to attend the fair without them. I was going to the big parade in downtown Dallas as well, which meant I'd have my first opportunity to use my pass and ride the city bus without a chaperone. I couldn't wait. I was prepared to eat lots of weird, fun foods and use all the coupons I would purchase enjoying the rides.

I soon learned there was a caveat to me riding the bus and attending the opening day parade. My parents would not allow me to go alone. I had to choose a friend from our neighborhood to hang out with whose parents were somewhat known by mine or I couldn't go. Problem was, the majority of my neighborhood school friends had already made plans with other friends since they had been going to the parade and fair without parental supervision for years. I was the late bloomer, a PK (preacher's kid) raised in a strict home being given permission for the first time to ride the city bus and attend the parade without my parents. The friend had to live in our neighborhood or I would not be allowed to go with them.

After speaking with several friends to find a bus and parade buddy, I was approached by a girl I grew up with. We lived on the same street for years while attending elementary school and my parents knew of her family, so we decided to run it by them. Much to my relief, my parents approved and made it clear that we were to ride the bus downtown together, attend the parade and come straight home afterward, no exceptions. I was happy, especially since this childhood friend had ridden the city bus and attended the parade a few times before. I considered her a pro.

For weeks, I patiently waited for opening day to arrive. The wait, in all of my childlike wonder, held the magic of a Christmas Eve night when you couldn't fall asleep fast enough so you could wake up and open your presents. In preparing for that day, I had already picked out my cutest outfit, just the right shoes and purse to compliment the outfit and decided how I would wear my long, thick hair. Back in the eighties, it was popular for girls to wear their hair straight and mine was flowing, so I was set to be super cute.

The weeks sped by and the day of the parade arrived. Genae's parents brought her to my home as planned. We had to sit for my mother's speech before we were allowed to leave. She reminded us to ride the bus to the parade and when it was over get back on the bus and come straight home. My mom told us not to take a ride from anyone whether we knew the person or not. Her point was well made. I understood very clearly since we asked to ride the bus, we were expected to ride the bus back home as well, no exceptions allowed. Excited, Genae and I headed out the door and walked down my block toward the bus stop to wait for the 31 Midway that would take us to downtown Dallas.

Like normal teenage girls, we laughed and talked the entire ride. I was fascinated with all the people crowding onto the bus headed downtown to the parade. Genae was like my personal tour guide, pointing out all the sights on the way there. It felt like we were on the bus forever when someone finally pulled the string sounding the bell. Genae said it was our stop. I smiled as we exited the bus onto the huge streets of downtown Dallas. Genae led the way since I knew nothing about walking downtown. I had only been downtown with my mother to drop off or pick up my dad from work at the Fairmont Hotel. Mom was a stay at home mother and Dad, a preacher, who also worked as a full-time chef.

The closer we got to the parade route, the louder the roar of the diverse crowd grew. Genae and I found a spot to stand and watched the bands and floats approaching. The hour-long parade was overwhelming. Once things appeared to be wrapping up, we started walking around looking at all the sights. I didn't mind walking. We stopped several times to talk with people we knew from the neighborhood or school. It was obvious we were killing time, but I didn't complain since it was my first unsupervised trip downtown. After a while, I asked Genae which direction we should head in order to catch the bus home. I didn't remember what street we'd gotten off at nor did I recall how far we had walked to get to the parade. I was lost.

When we finally reached the bus stop, she said the bus would be there in fifteen to twenty minutes. I couldn't have been more elated. My feet were beginning to hurt and I wanted to sit down.

The bus approached and we boarded. Just as we did in route to the parade, we started laughing and talking. After a few minutes, I noticed the sights did not look the same as before. I asked Genae if we were on the correct bus. She told me not to worry; she knew how to get us back home. I sat quietly and enjoyed the ride, but the longer we sat on the bus the more I worried Genae had us on the wrong bus. I thought perhaps she was too embarrassed to tell me.

The bus started turning onto streets I slightly remembered from my past. Before I knew it, we were on the west side of Dallas riding through a neighborhood my dad's church frequented to fellowship with other churches. I was about to ask Genae if she had us on the wrong bus, when she reached up and rung the bell for us to exit the bus. I knew some of my friends and classmates lived in this area so I wondered if perhaps she had friends in the area as well and decided to disobey my mom and visit them.

We exited the bus and Genae told me not to be scared. She said since we were so close to West Dallas, she needed to make a stop before we headed back to North Park and thought it best not to say anything because she knew my mom would not let me go with her. I was upset, but it was already getting late so I kept walking. We walked up to what looked like a big apartment building. Genae told me we were in the projects of West Dallas. You could never have prepared me for the direction this quick stop in West Dallas would take me.

2

Set Up By *My* Childhood Friend

We stood on a porch and Genae knocked on the door. I asked her whose house we were at and why we were there. She told me it was a friend of hers and that we wouldn't be there long, mentioning again she had to pick something up before we headed home. I was heated. I knew if my parents found out we didn't head home after the parade, I was going to be in big trouble. I was nervous about being somewhere I wasn't suppose to be with someone I didn't really know.

It felt like we knocked forever before a guy finally opened the door and told us to come in. The guy's face looked familiar and I wondered if I knew him from somewhere, but I couldn't fathom from where. He offered us a seat but I was uncomfortable being inside someone's house I did not know, so I remained standing. I was looking around, taking everything in when he offered us a seat again. This time, I sat.

The moment I sat down, Genae introduced me as her best friend. I thought to myself that's not true. You're just a girl from the neighborhood I grew up with and play sports with at school. You're not my best friend. The two of us never hung out or anything. This was the first time my parents had ever allowed me to go anywhere with a neighborhood friend alone outside of just hanging out at their house, and I was hardly ever allowed to do that. I had girlfriends from church and on rare occasions, I was allowed to sleep over their house.

But, Genae was definitely not one of those friends. Given the way I felt at that moment, she never would be.

The pictures on display in the living room helped me figure out where I had seen the guy. I was a member of the girls' junior varsity basketball team. At every game, the girls played, then the JV boys played, followed by the varsity team. This guy was a basketball player for LG Pinkston, one of our rival schools in West Dallas.

Even though I didn't know him personally, I had an idea of who the guy was. I was still confused about what Genae needed to pick up from his house. I wondered how she even knew him other than the fact that he played basketball for a rival team. Looking at pictures of him dressed in a cap and gown, I assumed he had either graduated already or was about to graduate.

I sat there with a stupid expression on my face while they conversed with one another. I was ready to go home, but Genae paid me no mind. Her entire demeanor said we didn't have to rush off. She started laughing and being silly with him.

I thought about leaving on my own, but I had no idea how to get around and I was afraid of being in the projects of West Dallas. People had stared at us as we walked through each huge building. I felt like an outsider that had landed somewhere I did not belong. Besides, I was more terrified of trying to figure out how to ride the city bus home alone.

Being raised as a sheltered girl in a strict Christian home, I was naïve about life outside my home, neighborhood, church and school. I kept wishing Genae would hurry up so we could catch the bus home. I knew I couldn't use the phone and call my parents. There was no way I could do that. I was more scared to do that than just sit and wait for her to hurry up. I couldn't even fathom calling my mom and telling her I was in the projects of West Dallas at some boy's house that Genae knew. I didn't even know exactly what housing project or street I was on. In my naïveté, I thought it would be better to wait until Genae was ready to leave.

I lost track of how long I sat looking at the walls while they talked before the two of them went into another room, obviously his room. They weren't in there long. When they came out, Genae said let's go. I thought FINALLY, we are going home. The guy grabbed his keys. I was curious about where he was going, and then assumed he was walking us to the bus stop. We walked between the different buildings and then up to another building. Exasperated, I wondered where were we going. I needed to get home. The guy knocked slightly on a door and then turned the knob to open the door. Apparently, it was a house he visited frequently. We walked in and they both sat down. I followed. Confused, I thought what now? I never opened my mouth to ask either of them what we were doing there. I sat quietly looking around. Eventually, a guy came downstairs and the guys walked away to talk. I whispered firmly to Genae that I needed to go home. She calmly responded that we were getting ready to go soon. The two guys returned to the living area. Introductions were made, but to be honest, I didn't hear what they said the guy's name was nor did I care. I just wanted to go home.

He was another familiar face of someone I didn't know. Genae's friend mentioned they both had played basketball together for LG Pinkston. I figured that must be where I had seen him before, though it didn't matter. I was ready to go home.

The day was getting late and I had reiterated to Genae I had to get home. Her friend whispered something to her and they stood. I stood as well and her friend looked at me weird. I asked Genae if she was ready to go. Her friend said he had forgotten to give her something from his house and they would be right back. I was furious and asked if we were walking all the way back over there. The other guy jumped in saying the bus stop was close to his house and I should make them walk over by themselves. As mad as I was, I told Genae to hurry up and come back so we could catch the bus home.

The guy Genae left me with seemed nice. He made small talk about school stuff, while I listened halfheartedly. He never knew I was upset and scared to death being in his house. It seemed like hours passed. He asked if he could show me some pictures he had been talking about and began walking up the stairs. Naïve and stupid, I timidly followed him. We walked into a bedroom and there were basketball pictures of him with his team. He mentioned he and the guy Genae was with had played together for years and that he was already out of high school. I was shocked. He asked me to sit down on his bed and started to shut the door. I immediately walked back closer to the door and asked him if we could please go back downstairs so I could wait on Genae. I had never been in a boy's personal space, had never been in a boy's house, and definitely not in a boy's room. I was nervous and uncomfortable.

He walked closer to me as I stood there pleading my case to go downstairs. All of a sudden, he closed the door shut. I wondered why he needed to shut the door in the first place. All kinds of questions popped into my head. Why was I here? Why did he want me to sit on his bed? Why did he shut the door? Where was Genae? I wondered why she was taking so long to return. As these thoughts raced through my mind, this guy suddenly turned me around from the door and sat me down on his bed. I started shaking. I was so confused. He said my friend was doing the same thing. I wondered what same thing he was referring to. What was it he thought I was doing? I had no idea what Genae was doing or what I should be doing. I asked him again to please let me go wait downstairs or even outside, but he ignored me.

Before I knew it, he was touching my body. I asked him to stop but he would not. I was unsure what was going on and why he wanted to touch me or how he felt he could. This boy didn't know me or know anything about me. What was he thinking? He was not listening to me nor would he stop. I was not prepared mentally, physically or emotionally for what he was doing to me or why he was doing it. All I knew was it needed to stop soon because I was scared to death.

I sat there in complete fear being touched by this boy, but I didn't fight back. I was so terrified all I could do was cry. He told me I would make it hard on myself if I didn't calm down. I didn't even understand what that meant. I just wanted to catch the bus and go home. He pushed me back onto his bed. I lay there motionless, as he pulled up my shirt and touched my bra. I cried even harder because I didn't understand why he would do this to a girl he had just met and did not know. I wondered if all older boys did this to girls they didn't know. And if so, why?

The only stupid thing I had done as a teenage girl was let a boy barely kiss me. If I thought a boy was going to try and touch me, I would hit him and let him know I was going to tell on him. At school, boys my age thought I was mean. They never really tried to go any further than acting like they wanted a kiss. I didn't know girls let boys do the kind of stuff this boy did to me. I didn't know how any of this worked. Surely this was not how it happened. I kept crying and crying as he touched all over my bra. Then, he exposed my breasts.

I closed my eyes and prayed the touching would stop so I could get up and go home. Instead, he put his hand inside my pants. I jumped and opened my eyes, begging him to please stop. He ignored me as if I had not uttered a word. Eventually, he said I would make it hurt if I didn't lie there and be still. I lay still again. I felt my pants being unzipped and pulled down. Filled with fear I thought, why am I here? Why me? He moved my legs apart, which not only hurt me, but embarrassed me as well. He was going to see my private area. I lay there crying and shut my eyes even tighter. He kept pushing my legs open to look at me, so I no longer resisted. I thought surely once he saw me it would all be over. He would let me up and I could finally go home. Everything seemed to happen in slow and fast motion all at the same time, which didn't make sense to me. I lay there, sobbing, praying he would stop and let me up.

I don't recall when, but all of a sudden I realized this boy had pulled his pants down because I felt what I knew as a boys' private part touching me. Horrified by his penis touching me, I thought I was going to be sick. My eyes were shut tight, but I could feel the tears flowing down my face. I kept thinking where is Genae? Maybe the other boy was doing her the same way and she was just as scared as I was. I wondered if Genae knew what was happening to me with this strange boy she had left me with. Surely, she could not know what he was doing to me. I felt so helpless. I was in a strange house in some strange boy's room, lying on his bed with my clothes half up and the other half down. I was embarrassed that he was touching me and could see me half naked. All I could think to do was cry. And that's what I did. I cried harder and harder.

I hoped he would be finish looking at me soon so he would leave me alone. I prayed for Genae to knock on the door so I could get up and go home. But, no one came and just when I thought it couldn't get any worse, it did.

Scared and totally unaware of what was going on, I was shaking and crying. I felt him pushing his private on my legs, which hurt me. I wondered what he was doing and began to push on his chest. He told me to stop or it would hurt worse. What could possibly hurt worse than this? He kept pushing harder. All of a sudden, his private went in between my legs. He had forced himself inside of my private area. I realized he was going to do the bad thing I had heard older kids did. All that time he was doing everything else, I never suspected he was going to have sex with me. The force of him penetrating me hurt me so bad. I tried closing my legs tight, but he kept pushing himself inside. It felt like I had been crying for hours when he finally said he was done. He walked away and left the room. I didn't think I would be able to move, but I managed to stand and quickly pull up my underwear. I had no recollection of him pulling them down. I pulled up my pants and fixed my shirt.

I was in a great amount of distress and wanted to throw up. I felt horrible...weak. Hearing him talking to someone, I wiped the tears from my face. I wondered who was down there. He told me to hurry up and come downstairs because my friend was on her way back. I figured he must have called them on the phone.

I gathered myself to walk down the stairs. The door opened and Genae and her friend walked in, talking. I demanded that she take me to the bus stop right away so I could go home. She could see I was upset. Her friend asked if he could give us a ride home and I told her no, we were going to take the bus home now. The boys were talking to each other as I walked out the door. Genae followed behind me this time. Her friend walked with us to the bus stop, but the other guy stayed at his house. It seemed as if we were there forever before a bus finally showed up.

I could see the two of them hugging and kissing before Genae entered the bus. Once we were seated on the bus, she looked out the window and waved at him, while I sat there in pain reflecting on what happened to me. It was clear to me my childhood friend whom I trusted to experience riding the city bus and attending the State Fair of Texas parade had set me up to be sexed by a stranger. At that time, I had no idea what the boy did to me was considered rape or sexual assault.

3

The Troubling *Bus* Ride Home

Still in shock, I was upset and extremely rattled. The only thing I wanted to do was get home, take a bath and go to bed. Genae started talking to me about her friend and how excited she was to see him again. She said that was the third time she had been able to see him and she was glad I came with her. Unlike earlier that day when I wanted to talk and ask lots of questions, I was absolutely speechless. All I could think about was the terrible thing that had happened. I didn't hear everything she said. She mentioned walking to his house and no one being at home so they hung out in his bedroom. I wondered if the same thing happened to her that happened to me, but she was happy and smiling while talking about the guy so I assumed it must have been very different for her.

As we passed by familiar places I remembered seeing in route to the parade, I felt a sense of comfort knowing I would be home soon. I wondered if Genae could tell by looking at me what the boy had done. I got really scared thinking if she could tell my parents would be able to tell. I kept thinking about how much trouble I was going to be in because we were late and my parents might be able to look at me and tell I had sex.

Genae finally stopped talking about how happy she was and asked if I liked the boy they had picked out for me to hang with. She said he use to be a popular basketball player from LG Pinkston. I told her I hadn't come to hang out with any boys and my parents were going to get me if they found out. She asked me another question and I started crying uncontrollably. Put off by my outburst, she looked around to see if anyone else was watching me. To my knowledge, no one else was. She asked if I was okay. I told her I was extremely angry with her for tricking me into going to the projects of West Dallas and that I did not like the fact that she took me to someone's home I didn't know and then had the nerve to leave me there by myself. In my verbal explosion, I let Genae know he made me have sex with him while she was gone.

Genae wasn't sympathetic to my being upset. She was more concerned about me telling my parents where we had been and about what happened to me. I told her I didn't want anyone to know what that boy had done to me, especially my parents. My dad would have killed him. Since we were late returning home, she concocted a story to tell our parents. She said we would tell them we were separated from one another in the crowd and when we finally met up, we accidentally took the wrong bus and had to find our way back downtown to catch the 31 Midway. She was confident this would keep us from being in too much trouble and give us a reason for making it back home so late. I was convinced this was not the first time Genae had done this. She seemed to have all the answers.

As mad as I was with her, I decided that would be the best thing and agreed to never mention anything about us going to the projects of West Dallas or stopping at those boys' houses instead of getting on the bus coming directly back home.

I had calmed down enough to talk. I asked Genae did she lie about having to pick something up so she could see that boy. She admitted she lied. There was nothing for her to pick up. She said she didn't want to go to the projects by herself and knew it was the only way for her to get me to go with her. Genae informed me her boyfriend, who I knew nothing about, said since she was bringing a friend with her, he would get one of his friends to let me hang out at his house so they could go off by themselves and have sex. Now, I hated both of those boys. I wanted to be certain I had heard her clearly, so I asked her if she took me out there knowing she was going to have sex and that her friend was setting me up to be around a boy alone. She told me yes she knew. Genae felt it necessary to let me know they had had sex a few times and she liked being with him. I decided that day I would never go anywhere with her ever again in my life and I never did. How could this girl take me over a boy's house she knew wanted me for sex? Even if she didn't know, she was as much to blame as her friend who knew his intentions for having Genae bring a girl with her. She knew I was not that type of girl. I had no clue about having sex. I had never done anything to Genae. I was nice to people. I volunteered to help others out at school. For her to participate in setting me up like that confused me. I felt used and stupid.

The bus seemed to be moving slower and slower. All I wanted to do was get home. Genae stated with pride that she liked having sex with that boy. She asked me if it was my first time. I told her I had never had sex before, didn't know how and never wanted to know how. I told Genae that boy hurt me so bad and that I cried the entire time. She said she didn't think I would be that upset and I should have just told him to stop. If I was the type to fight, which I was not, I could have hit her in the face. Every response she gave made me angrier. I told her I had asked him to leave me alone the very first time he touched me. I even begged him to let me go back downstairs or outside to wait for her to come back, but he told me I was going to make it hurt worse and I had no clue what he was talking about. I told Genae the only thing I had ever done with one boy was let him kiss me. She laughed, which made me even more upset. I told her everything that happened to me was all her fault and I no longer wanted to hang out with her ever again in my life. I was never mean to people, but I went ahead and told her exactly how I felt about her. She said from the look on my face at his house she didn't think I liked him that much and she was sorry if I did not like the boy they picked for me to hang with that day.

Genae had no idea how I truly felt nor did she seem to care. I told her when we arrived at my house I would have my mom take her home and the two of us would never speak about this again. When the bus turned on Kenwell Street, our conversation stopped. We exited the bus and walked toward my house in dead silence. I was furious with her and she was mad at me, for what I didn't know. We arrived at my house pretending to be jovial. After we told my mom we got lost in the crowd and had to take a late bus home, she was no longer upset and wanted to hear about my first bus ride downtown and what I thought about the parade.

I faked a smile and told my mom about the bus ride, parade, walking downtown and who I ran into that she knew. She was glad I had a good time and asked if I wanted to see if Genae could sleep over. I said no, I was tired and did not want her to stay over which made Genae look at me funny. My mom told her to call her parents and see if they were home. Her parents were home so we jumped in the car. When we arrived at Genae's house, she opened the door and got out while I sat there. My mom told me to get out and thank her parents for letting her go with me. I kept wondering if my mom was able to tell I had sex. I prayed to God that she wouldn't ask me any questions.

Once I got back in the car, my mom asked if everything was okay. I said it was, that I was exhausted from the long bus rides, walking downtown at the parade and the stress of getting lost. I told her all I wanted to do was take a bath and go to bed. She said she understood. Inside, I sighed with deep relief. I was home and hoped I could forget everything that happened to me. My first ride on the city bus downtown had turned out to be the worst day of my fifteen-year-old life.

Sex was something I heard very little about in my young life; something I was never prepared to have anytime soon...if ever. I wanted to wait until I got married like the women at my church who were my role models. I had no desire to have a boyfriend and the few boys that tried kissing me were turned off by my lack of interest, which was completely okay by me. What a horrible day. I prayed God would let me forget it forever.

4

Keep It To Yourself, No One Will Ever Know

We returned home and I went straight to my room, picked out my bedclothes and prepared for a bath. My spirit was low, but I had to pretend everything was okay since I was home. I gathered my clothes, went to start the water and did the normal thing of going around the house to see if anyone had to use the restroom. We were not fortunate enough to have more than one bathroom in our home; therefore it was a rule to make sure no one needed to use the facility before you locked the door to bathe. Both of my parents were good and each of my four siblings gave me thumbs up signaling they were all good.

My parents had five children. My brother was the oldest and the only boy. We spoiled him. I was three years younger than my older brother and the oldest girl in the family. The other girls fell in line one after the other with a two-year gap separating the younger two. We grew up extremely close-knit and, for the most part, got along very well. Our parents taught us to look out for each other. We never got into trouble at school, church or in the neighborhood because we didn't want to embarrass our parents. My dad raised us with a healthy respect for the word fear. We knew not to bring disappointment to our home for our parents to deal with.

We didn't pretend to be perfect and were never raised to think such a thing. Our parents had a very tight rein on us so getting into trouble was pretty much non-existence for my siblings and I. We went to school and church. Occasionally, we were allowed to stay overnight with a family member or close friend. I thought my parents were pretty overprotective. They never allowed us to do anything unless it was a church or family function. We were surprised they gave us permission to participate in school sports which most of us did. Being able to attend the State Fair parade with a friend and going on my first city bus ride was a huge step for them. After what happened to me, I understood their decision a little more. It had to be because they didn't want us to experience such horrific things like I had experienced. Being away from the safety of my siblings and parents was definitely not worth it. If that was what other children did with a little bit of freedom, I wasn't interested. I would rather stick with the life I was accustomed to: church, school, church, school, church, school.

I ran my bath water and undressed, pausing to use the bathroom before sitting in the tub. I stepped into the tub, sat down and began crying very quietly. I didn't want any of my siblings to hear me because they would tell Mom and she would ask why I was crying. I remember thinking I had to scrub my private area real hard because I felt nasty and I was still hurting from what that boy did to me. Once I finished bathing, I stepped out of the tub and noticed my underwear had stains on them. I picked them up, startled to see small spots of blood. I knew I would really be in trouble. My mom would know I had sex with a boy because my menstrual cycle was coming back. I was terrified of becoming sick after seeing the blood because I had taken a bath instead of a shower and baths were forbidden when you were on your period.

I stood in the bathroom trying to figure out how I could explain to Mom I needed sanitary napkins again after my menstrual cycle had recently ended. Crying harder, I thought for sure someone would hear me, but no one did. I took a few sanitary napkins out of the cabinet and hid them underneath my bedclothes until I made it back to my room. All I wanted to do was go to sleep. I swore no one would ever know what happened to me besides Genae. Those two boys didn't know my family or any of my friends so I could care less about them. I was confident there was no one those boys would tell nor would Genae. At least, I prayed she didn't.

I thought about telling my brother because he could keep a secret. I trusted him more than anyone else in the world, but I was too embarrassed to tell him. How could I tell my brother what happened? As close as he and I were, I was afraid he would tell our parents and I couldn't take that chance.

I rushed to put on my bedclothes and made sure to secure my sanitary napkin. That boy had hurt me so bad he made my menstrual cycle start early and I had to wear a sanitary pad again. I hated wearing pads. As I gathered my things to exit the bathroom, my mom met me at the door. Could she tell I had sex? Would she be able to tell I was having my period again? Why else would I get my period so quickly when I had just had it two or three weeks ago? Thankfully, Mom only needed to use the bathroom. I proceeded to my room and hid the extra sanitary pads in my drawer. I got on my knees to say my prayers as we were raised to do. I really needed God to give me some peace. I hated my period. I was hurting from the boy forcing himself inside me and I felt bad, but it didn't feel the same way as when my period normally started. The cramps were missing.

I lay in bed trying to fall asleep, but I kept seeing that boy's face in my mind. I could see him touching me and pulling my clothes away to expose my private parts. I couldn't figure out what I had done to make Genae pick me to be the girl she would take with her to be sexed by a boy. I hated her whether she knew he intended to force sex on me or not. Genae never should have placed me in that situation especially since she had no clue if I was capable of defending myself. I thought she wanted us to become close friends, but that was all a lie. She wanted to use me, which she had succeeded in doing in the worst way. I also hated those two boys whose names I couldn't even remember. Why would they do that to me, especially the boy who had me crying while he forced himself on me? He didn't know anything about me and I didn't know him. Why would you trick a girl you just met into your room and force her to lay there while you had sex with her? Why? I was so confused. I couldn't even remember what the boy looked like. I recalled him being proud of his basketball pictures. I laid awake for hours, head spinning. I still had no idea why all three of them decided to pick me. Even if I wanted to tell my brother or my parents, they would think I was crazy for not knowing the boy's name. I couldn't show them where he lived or anything. All I knew was his house was one of the large apartment buildings in the housing projects of West Dallas. I remembered seeing a funny street name Delhi as we were leaving, but that would not help direct me back over there to show anyone.

How was I going to find out anything about this boy to tell my brother or my parents? I was sure Genae would lie about the entire day so she wouldn't get in trouble. I convinced myself to leave it alone. That was it; I decided. No one would ever know. As the old phrase went, I would take this one to my grave.

The more I thought about it, I thought maybe I would tell. I deliberated on the thought long and hard and then settled in my mind. I was 100% sure I was going to keep this secret to myself. NO ONE would ever know what happened. I was scared no one would believe me since I didn't tell Mom right away. I eventually fell asleep but woke up later to go check my pad. It was dry. I didn't understand how that could be. There had been blood in my underwear, however nothing was on the pad or in the toilet. What kind of menstrual cycle was I experiencing? I was naïve and had no understanding about what happened to me. I woke up the next morning, still nothing on my sanitary pad. I was happy and confused. I decided to play it safe and wore a dreadful pad all day.

5

School *Is* My Therapy

Sunday was a normal day like any other. We attended church. The sanitary pad was dry as well so I began to think maybe he had only hurt me bad enough to make my period start for a day. My mom asked several times if anything was wrong, but I played it off. I kept going to the bathroom more than normal just to check my pad. Every time I checked, it was still dry. I was terrified to take it off because I didn't want to mess up my clothes. We ate Sunday dinner, watched television and prepared for the school week. I was anxious to get in bed and went earlier than normal, telling Mom I was still tired from my busy day at the parade.

Monday arrived and I was ready to head off to school. I needed to avoid my mom. I was afraid my looks, the way I was behaving or being on my period again so quickly would give me away. In class, I drifted off several times remembering everything that happened. I felt like my secret was on display and everyone looking at me could tell. I was nervous the entire day. Usually, I saw Genae at school and was relieved when I didn't see her. I was excited about volleyball practice after school. I hoped it would take my mind off my first unexpected, horrible experience with sex.

I entered the locker room to change and thought it prudent to go check my pad. The sanitary pad was still dry so I took it off and prayed my period was over. I was sure Genae did not come to school because she also played volleyball and was not there for practice. I focused on practice and blocked out everything that had happened. Any other day, our practice seemed to last forever. That day, it went by too fast. I carpooled with another girl from the neighborhood. Once I got home, I had to bathe, do homework and eat dinner. I did the family roll call regarding the bathroom then started my bath water while I gathered my clothes. I examined my underwear thoroughly. There was still no blood, which made me happy. I figured since I only saw stains on the day the boy forced sex on me, maybe my period was already over and decided against putting on another pad.

The next few days, I followed the same routine. Going to school was the best thing ever, mainly because volleyball practice allowed me to focus on something else. It helped a lot that Genae was not at school, that way I didn't have to deal with her. Her missing school did not bother me at all. I never picked up the phone to call and check on her either. I actually could have cared less if she ever came back to school. Eventually, Genae would come back to school and although I told her to never talk to me again, I knew that wouldn't last with that girl. We were on the same team and would have to talk to each other at least at practice and for the games. Genae was away from school for three days. Her first day back, she didn't say anything to me. That Friday, she asked to speak to me, but I was hesitant. Since she asked, I decided to listen to what she had to say, thinking she was going to apologize.

We didn't have practice after school, so Genae asked me to sit with her on the school bus home so we could talk. I accepted. Once we got on the bus, she told me she was out of school for three days because she and her boyfriend had an argument so she told her mom she was sick. I didn't care about him or her and it was obvious by my facial expression. She wanted to know if I would accept her apology for tricking me into going to the projects of West Dallas and leaving me at that boy's house alone. I was hurt and still upset about the entire situation so I told her I would think about it. I just knew I no longer wanted to hang around her because I didn't think I could ever get past what she did. Genae said her boyfriend asked if I was mad at his friend and inquired if I had told anyone. I informed her that I was very upset with all three of them and had no intention of telling anyone what the boy did to me. I expressed my embarrassment to her and told her I just wanted it all to go away. She said hopefully she and I could be friends again and hang out at each other's house. I told her I was not interested and didn't need or want friends like her. The bus ride was short. After we arrived in our neighborhood, I exited the bus first and told her goodbye. She told me to have a nice weekend.

Over the next few weeks, I constantly thought about how that boy violated me. I still had not told anyone. I believed the best thing to do was enjoy school, try not to think about it and hope it would stop popping up in my mind. Genae and I were cordial, speaking to each other during practice and games, no more no less. She understood now how truly upset and hurt I was and that I was not willing to accept her apology or pretend like nothing happened. I was taught in church to always forgive people, however I was not ready to do that with her.

Winter break was fast approaching and I was excited about the upcoming holidays. Attending school and being actively involved in sports kept me occupied, but I loved our school breaks. Being in school was my own little personal therapy. I could tell school was a distraction from the incident in early October. I did have mixed feelings about being on break for two weeks around Mom and my siblings. I feared Mom would somehow be able to tell what happened and I would finally have to explain everything to her.

Before we left on winter break, Genae wanted to talk to me again. She asked if we could ride the school bus home together so we could talk in private. I felt like she was ignoring the fact that I did not wish to talk to her or maybe she was going to try really hard to push me to be her friend again. Either way, I accepted her invite to talk. She asked me again if I was still upset with her. I told her yes, this was not something I would ever forget and to be honest, I would not hate her forever because I was taught at church if someone does anything bad, God expects you to forgive them, but that didn't mean I would hang out with her again. Genae blurted out she had a surprise for me. I knew whatever it was would never make up for what happened. As we approached our neighborhood, we passed her stop and she stayed on the bus. I wondered what she wanted so badly that she would miss her stop.

Once we approached my street, I got up to exit the bus and she followed. I inquired as to where she was going. She said she had something for me and needed to tell me something before we went on break. I had no clue what she could possibly have to give or tell me. As we were walking, she asked me to stop so I did. Genae gave me a piece of paper that was folded up and smiled really hard. I asked her what it was. She told me I was going to be happy. The look on my face was one of total confusion. Why would I be happy with anything from her? I asked her to tell me what it was and explain to me why I was going to be so happy. Her response completely blindsided me.

Genae asked me to open the paper first before she told me the good news. I unfolded the piece of paper to see the name Clint and a phone number. I was speechless. I didn't have a clue about what I held in my hand. She was smiling really hard like I should know this person. She asked if I was happy now and I replied, happy about what. I didn't even know who this was. She informed me it was the guy I met in the projects of West Dallas. He had told her boyfriend he wanted to see me again. I was in shock. Why would she think I would be happy or even want to see this boy ever again? I lost it.

I was not happy he wanted to talk to me after what he did. I started yelling that I didn't care anything about this boy. I told her he probably wanted to do the same thing to me and that was never going to happen. I was not interested in seeing him, talking to him or going to his house ever again in my life. I asked her if she had forgotten what happened to me. Without waiting for her response, I told her that boy tricked me into his room to see pictures, pulled down my clothes and put his private inside me and hurt me real bad. This boy had me crying while he forced his penis inside me and I never wanted to see his face again.

I continued to yell at Genae that she and her friend were the reason it all happened. I reminded her they set me up and were both at fault for taking me to his house and leaving me there alone. I informed her they knew why they wanted me in West Dallas that day and most likely had a clear idea of what he wanted to do to me and that was unforgiveable. I told Genae to tell her boyfriend and this Clint boy I was never going to see him or call him and if he didn't leave me alone, I would tell my brother. She stood there looking stupid, so I told her that was it. I was done being her friend and although I was raised to forgive, I was never in my life going to forgive her. She was never to speak to me again in or out of school and I meant it. I didn't want to ride the bus with her and she was never to come by my house for anything. I was done with her for good. The nerve of her to think I wanted to call or see that boy again. I turned to walk home and left her standing on the sidewalk looking foolish. She never tried calling out to me, which was probably the best thing she could have done that day.

As I walked toward my house I could feel myself about to explode. I needed to calm down before I actually reached the house. I didn't want to give my mom any reason to ask questions because I knew I would burst into tears. The piece of paper with the boy's name and phone number was still in my hand so I folded it up and stuck it inside my purse. Why I did that instead of tearing it up and throwing it away I can't explain. I reached our yard and composed myself before I entered the house. After having it out with Genae, I could finally put this all behind me. I had to work on trying to forget about being sexually assaulted so I could move on with my tenth grade life. This was a lot for a fifteen year old to keep inside. However, in my head, I thought that was the best solution. I was so ashamed and felt strong enough to deal with it on my own.

I was glad it was the final day of school before winter break. I could avoid Genae for the next two weeks as I worked on getting myself together before returning to school in January.

6

Is This Secret *Making* My Body Sick?

During winter break, we slept in late and enjoyed the holidays and time off from school with our family. I stuck to my word and did not speak to Genae once we returned to school in January. Actually, we both avoided each other. Even though I started to feel a little better about myself, I still had those dark sad moments when the thought of what took place weighed heavily inside my mind, body and soul. There were only a few days where the thought of that horrible day in the fall of 1981 didn't cross my mind. On days where it weighed heaviest, I coped by keeping busy.

Besides attending high school, I was heavily involved in church. I sang in the choir, attended youth bible class, went to prayer service or babysat. In our home, there was no staying at home if the church doors were open. Being a preacher's family, we went to everything.

My siblings and I were part of a gospel family singing group with several of my uncles from my dad's side of the family. Several of my family members were gifted in singing and playing various instruments, including my brother who was one of our musicians. Two wealthy ladies had heard us sing somewhere and decided to invest in producing a gospel music album for our singing group to record. Over winter break, we spent time rehearsing for the studio recording that would take place in June. I was incredibly busy from mid-January until late February, then one week while enjoying my busy life something went terribly wrong.

By late February, I was not feeling well. I thought I had come down with a bad cold, virus or perhaps the flu. I was exhausted. I didn't have an appetite and my entire body felt sore. I was not a student who missed school days, practice or games and I absolutely enjoyed going to class, so I still went to school even though I had been feeling awful. One Friday morning, I woke up feeling horrible. I didn't care if I missed everything. I figured one absence on my attendance record would not be a big deal. I was running a fever, throwing up and tired as crap. I informed my mom I had the worst cramps ever and felt really weak when I tried to sit up or walk around.

My mom told me there was no way she would allow me to attend school like that and said we had to let whatever virus this was get out of my system. I stayed home and Mom consoled me by trying different things to help me feel better.

I didn't feel any better as the day went on and was forced to stay in the house all day Saturday. By evening, I felt a little better and was able to keep a little food down. I asked Mom if I could attend church. She said I would have to wait and see how I felt the next morning. I had been lying around for two days and was anxious and excited to get out of the house and go to church.

Sitting in church, I felt like I was going to be sick. I tried really hard to calm myself down hoping and praying it would pass. All of a sudden, I had to jump up and run to the bathroom. One of the ushers came in to check on me. She immediately left to get my mom because I was throwing up and complaining of having horrible pains.

Mom instructed me to lay in the choir room and rest since Dad was in the middle of his sermon. After service, we headed home, but Dad had to pull the car over because I got sick again before we made it home. Finally, we pulled into our driveway. The vomiting had subsided so I was able to change my clothing and rest on the couch in the family room where Mom watched over me.

I sipped on 7-Up, but everything I drank came back up. I asked my mom to please not give me anything else to drink and she agreed.

By Sunday evening, I was experiencing the same symptoms I had on Friday. My fever was high, my body ached horribly, and I was dry heaving. I was scared. My mind was racing out of control. I thought trying to keep my incident a secret for so long was making me sick. I wondered if God was punishing me for the horrible sin that happened to me early last October. I had been working hard for five months to get over that day and it was on my mind again as if it had happened yesterday. I thought for sure I was being punished for not telling my parents and God was causing me to be sick so He could force me to tell them.

I overheard my parents having a conversation about me being so sick. I could see the nervous, concerned expressions on their faces. To my recollection, I had never been that sick a day in my short fifteen years of life.

I recall Dad asking Mom if she thought I should go to the doctor that night. I could tell he was worried. My mom said if I didn't feel better the next morning, she would take me to the doctor to get checked out. I know they were praying none of the other four children became ill. I was sure my mom was fearful of having five of us throwing up and being feverish at the same time.

Monday morning came; the other kids prepared for school. They were all concerned about why I was so sick and what could be wrong with me, hoping they did not get sick. Mom told me I was not going to school. I didn't put up a fight about it at all because I felt terrible and wanted this to go away even if it meant missing school and going to the doctor. I was definitely not feeling better and had not slept most of the night, which kept Mom up. Dad and Mom agreed I had to see a doctor immediately, no more waiting. I had started feeling better and was no longer throwing up, but my entire body was still in a lot of pain. I was experiencing severe cramps in my back, side and stomach.

After Mom made sure the other kids were prepared to walk out the door to the local elementary school or catch the neighborhood school bus, she made a few phone calls. Mom told me to get dressed so she could take me to see a doctor. I struggled with getting dressed because of the cramps. I had never experienced cramps that bad before. I was anxious to see what type of medicine the doctor would prescribe to make everything go away.

Once everyone was gone, Mom and I drove to the county hospital. That made me nervous. I thought Mom was not telling me something and wondered if they were going to admit me. I was scared Mom was going to make them keep me and asked her why she brought me to the hospital. Naïve, I didn't realize the hospital also had a clinic. I panicked a little at the thought of having to be checked-in. Despite my emotional turmoil, we made it inside and Mom headed in the direction of the clinic. It was obvious she had been there before and knew her way around, but the more we walked the more nervous I became.

7

The Hospital's Shocking *News*, So Now We Wait

We finally made it to the clinic. There seemed to be hundreds of people waiting to see a doctor. I thought we would be there all day. We walked up to wait in a long line and were handed paperwork to complete. Once we made it to the counter, the lady asked a few questions and directed us to fill out the forms, telling us to bring them back to the counter when they were complete. I thought it was a lot of paperwork just to see a doctor. We found chairs and Mom quickly filled out the paperwork. A little weak from the walk, Mom let me stay seated to save our chairs and took the paperwork to the counter.

They reviewed the forms, gave Mom a number and told her which clinic to take me to, instructing us to listen for our number. We headed to another area of the hospital. It appeared the system they used moved people fairly quickly. Thankfully, not everyone was headed in the same direction or to the same clinic. We took the elevator to another floor and found the clinic we needed. When we got there they asked Mom several questions. Some of them I had to answer about how I was feeling at the time. A nurse took me into a room to get my vital signs and advised me they would be drawing blood and doing a urine test. She told us since I was not able to answer some of her questions, they would run a few routine tests.

We sat in the waiting area with everyone else until my name was called. I headed to the counter where a lady handed me a cup to get a urine sample then advised she would be doing blood work. I hated peeing in a cup, although I was use to collecting urine for my sport physicals, I thought it was the nastiest and weirdest thing to do. After I finished, I placed the cup where instructed, and followed the nurse into a room where she drew my blood. Even though the needle stung, I was okay with getting blood drawn more than collecting urine in a cup. I completed those two tasks and went back to the waiting area.

I was feeling a little better which made me somewhat relieved. I asked Mom what they would do next. She said they would call me into a room and check me out.

While we waited, I fell asleep with my head in Mom's lap. The lack of sleep from the night before had finally caught up with me. Mom shook me and said they were calling my name. It felt as if I had been sleep for hours. We got up and headed to meet the lady holding my chart. She told us the doctor was waiting on my lab results, in the meantime she needed me to undress, put on a gown and wait for the doctor to come in. Mom said she would step out so I could get undressed. I thought she was going to stay in the room and she clearly saw the embarrassment on my face. I was shy taking off my clothes even in my own home unless I was in the bathroom or alone in my room.

I put the gown on quickly and giggled to myself. As I sat and waited, Mom knocked on the door. I told her she could come back inside. I told Mom the lady had me leave the open part of the gown in the front. She convinced me the gown was on correctly. We sat there talking when a doctor finally walked in with a gentle knock on the door to announce himself. The doctor introduced himself to us and took a seat. He informed us he had been reviewing my chart and needed to ask some questions. He went over some routine things about my height, weight and other vitals and then stated he was waiting on my blood work. He said he had ordered the results to be rushed from the lab. I didn't quite understand everything he said, but I became nervous when he said there was a rush on my blood work. I wondered if there was a specific reason why they had rushed the blood work.

The doctor was very nice when asking questions and allowed Mom to answer for me when he saw I was not able to respond. After a few minutes, someone knocked on the door. Unlike the doctor, they waited until he said come in. It was the nurse who had taken my urine and blood. She advised him my "stat" blood work was back and asked him to step outside.

The doctor told us he would be back in a few minutes then he and the nurse left the room. Mom and I looked worried as we sat there waiting for them to return. Even at fifteen, I could tell something was not right and Mom's face confirmed it without her saying anything to me. We didn't understand what could be wrong or why they left the room to discuss my blood work.

Just when the room could not have been more silent, the doctor walked in gently knocking and opening the door at the same time just as before. He said again that he needed to ask me a few more questions and then would need to examine me. I remember sitting there frightened to death wondering what was wrong with me. What had they found in my blood work? When would they tell us? Was I getting ready to die? Was that why I had been so sick? The doctor asked me when my last menstrual cycle was. I told him I had my period last month, but couldn't recall the actual date. He then asked if I had been sexually active. I lied and said no. My heart started racing really fast. I felt like I was going to throw up.

I wondered why the doctor was asking me about sex. Could he tell what happened to me five months ago from my "stat" blood work? Did that boy give me a disease when he forced me to have sex? Before I knew it, tears streamed down my face. I thought my mom was going to find out about that boy. The way the doctor questioned me I figured that boy must have given me a disease and made me real sick. I sat there with my head down, crying. The doctor told me everything was going to be okay. He said he needed me to be totally honest with him. I knew at that moment, the doctor realized I was not being honest about having sex. He didn't know it was not my fault. I couldn't tell him what happened in front of my mom. I was not going to say anything. It was apparent the doctor already knew something happened to me sexually from my blood work. I was scared and embarrassed for not being able to speak the truth to the doctor as my mom sat there, looking sad.

The doctor offered me tissue to wipe my tears and told me to calm down before I upset myself more. He stayed in the room the entire time I was breaking down. Mom and I still had no clue what disease I had. We just knew it had to be pretty bad for the doctor to be so concerned. Once I was able to calm down, the doctor said he needed to examine me to confirm something. I didn't understand the medical terms he used. Mom told him that would be fine and said she would step out of the room if I wanted her to, which I did. I didn't know what he would be examining, but I knew since I had this gown on it had to be my body and I was shy. I had no idea what Mom was thinking or why she agreed to step out the room so quickly, but she did. The doctor had the nurse come back inside and she began getting things out of a drawer for him. I wondered what I could possibly have and what were they preparing to do to me during this exam?

I was told to sit on the table, then the nurse told me to lie down. As I did, tears started to stream down my face again and they both asked if I was okay. I told them I was scared. The doctor said I was not the first young girl to be dishonest to their parents about having sex and that I should always talk to them or an adult I could trust. I was good talking with the doctor and nurse for some odd reason, maybe because they didn't know me. I felt safe enough to tell them I didn't know anything about having sex nor did I plan to have sex. I told them a boy I didn't know made me lie down and be still while he had sex with me. They both advised me to discuss that with my mom. I thought I would finally have to tell Mom what happened to me. As much as I made myself believe I would never have to discuss that horrible day again, here I was facing an illness forced with telling my parents what happened on the day I went to the State Fair of Texas parade with Genae.

The doctor and nurse began the examination. They had me take my arms out of the gown so they could squeeze each breast. I didn't understand why they were doing that. I felt so weird and continued to cry. The nurse put a sheet over me, lifted up my gown and said I would need to take my underwear off in a minute. I wondered what for, but I didn't ask. The doctor started pushing around on my sides and stomach asking me if anything hurt. Nothing did except my feelings. The nurse told me to slip off my underwear. She helped me not to fall off the table as I did.

She told me to slide down to the end of the table. When I did, I heard her making a bunch of noise. She positioned the sheet over my legs and started telling me she was placing my feet inside something and not to be alarmed. I was very alarmed and whatever I had my feet in was extremely cold. The doctor began talking me through everything he was doing, step by step. All of a sudden, I felt his hand going inside my private area. I didn't understand what he was doing or why. I cried even harder. He asked if he was hurting me or if I was just scared. I told him both.

It was extremely uncomfortable as I lay there being examined by this doctor. Even though he was very gentle with me, my mind thought I was being violated. The examination sent me back into that horrible day five months ago when I was taken advantage of in the worst way by that boy. When the exam was over, I was able to relax. They helped me off the table and the nurse gave me some tissue to wipe myself before I got dressed. As I dressed, I was thinking they would finally tell Mom and I what was wrong with me. All I wanted to know was what horrible disease or illness that boy had given me when he forced sex on me back in October. After I dressed, Mom came back into the room. She was very quiet, so was I. We did not say a word to each other.

We sat there for what seemed like hours. Mom broke the silence and asked me if there was something I needed to tell her. She told me not to be scared. I told her she already knew what happened and that I didn't want talk about it right then. I was still convinced I would never talk about it. I prayed they could give me medicine for whatever was making me sick. I just wanted to feel better. The now familiar gentle knocking and opening of the door interrupted my thoughts. The doctor entered the room by himself with my chart in his hand. As he sat down, my heart was beating faster than ever. Mom and I had been waiting to finally know what was wrong and what could be done to help make me better, if I was not dying already.

The doctor told Mom I was a good patient during the examination. He said the nurse was gathering some items for us to take home to review and would assist me in scheduling a follow-up visit to the clinic. Fifteen and super naïve, I wondered what he was talking about. I wanted to scream, "Just tell me!" The doctor said the labs from my urine and the blood work came back positive for pregnancy. PREGNANCY! WHO was pregnant? I held my head down and started to cry softly as he continued talking. He said due to something in my blood, he was required to do a physical examination. Based upon the results of the blood work and the physical examination, he was able to confirm that I was approximately five months pregnant with a due date of mid to late June. I started crying loud and hard. ME pregnant! I would rather he had told me I was dying.

I glanced around to look at Mom's face. She wasn't crying, but her face was sad and full of understanding at the same time. I remember her saying everything was going to be fine. She asked the doctor how I could have menstrual cycles every month and be pregnant. The doctor kindly explained although it was rare it did happen to some women. I was not a woman! How could this be? I was just a girl. Mom then inquired as to why I did not look pregnant and why had I not experienced any weight gain to reflect what was happening to my body. The doctor explained that while no weight gain and no physical changes to my body were rare, the test confirmed a viable pregnancy and that I was five months along. This doctor was telling us that I was carrying a baby inside of me. In a few months, I would be having a baby. In utter disbelief, we were SHOCKED.

Mom thanked him for his patience with me and for explaining everything to us.

We waited for the nurse to bring the information so we could check out and go home. I was not looking forward to going home. I remember thinking, God this can't really be happening to me, could it? How could You allow such a horrible act to ruin my life forever?

8

I Am Not Talking, So *Leave* Me Alone/My Shut Down

Total DISBELIEF! That is what I thought as Mom and I left the examining room that February day. I continued to cry as we collected the papers from the nurse. I was sad and angry. Most of what the nurse told Mom and I was foreign to me. Pregnant was the one word I definitely understood. I kept thinking over and over again, they just told me I was pregnant. And only I knew it was by a boy whose name I did not know that forced me to have sex with him. I thought my dad would kill me. Then I thought about how everyone would stare and talk about me for having sex and getting pregnant. No one would ever really know I didn't have sex by choice. Even if I told anyone, I didn't think they would believe me since I waited so long to say something. Only Genae who set me up that day and that boy knew the truth. Why had this happened to me? I was not perfect by any means, but I had never gotten into any trouble of this magnitude. The most I did was argue with my siblings about dumb stuff and my dad was not having that so we always made up quickly. I was extremely naïve and INNOCENT about worldly things unlike Genae who was purposely having sex with boys and enjoyed it. I hated that girl. She had ruined my life.

As we started walking down the hallway to leave the clinic, I felt dizzy. It was a long walk to my parent's car. I could tell Mom didn't know what to say to me or if she should say anything, so we walked in silence. I cried all the way to the car and once we got inside Mom told me again that everything was going to be fine. For the first time since leaving the clinic, I opened my mouth and asked if she had to tell Daddy. I was thinking about his reaction. What was my dad going to think about me or do to me? None of us five children had ever brought shame or embarrassment to our parents. I was ashamed of myself for having to tell my dad this bad news.

Mom asked if I wanted to talk about it and I said no. My mom never pushed the issue as to who, where, when, or why. I'm sure some people might wonder why my mom did not demand answers to her questions or force her fifteen-year-old daughter to talk. Perhaps it was just her way. The only thing my mom ever told us regarding boys was that girls keep their dresses down, nothing else. We never asked what that meant nor did my mom go into detail to explain that statement. My mom didn't even talk to us girls about how a menstrual cycle worked. I found out later in life, she did me the exact way her mom did, or worse. My mom let me learn by myself, which meant I knew nothing. I was twelve years old when my menstrual cycle started and never had a conversation with my mom about it. One day after walking home from school in the sixth grade, instead of going outside to play like all the other kids, I went to my room and got in the bed. Mom came to the room like she knew I had started my period.

The only thing I remember her asking that day was if it came on at school and if I had messed up my clothes. I told her it had and that my clothes were not messed up. Mom took me in the bathroom and explained how to put on a sanitary napkin. She told me my cycle would last about four to five days. I thought to myself, why and what for, but I never asked any questions and she didn't offer more information or details than that.

I don't blame my mom for her lack of parenting skills. I suppose she did what she knew and handled things like her mom did. Besides that, my mom left school in the tenth grade to marry my father at the age of fifteen. So maybe she really didn't know much more than I did at that age. For the record, she was not a teenage mom. She actually married my dad for love as a virgin. Although I was the oldest girl, Mom never instructed me to let her know if my period was abnormal. I had no clue what an abnormal period was anyway. If every month over the past five months I didn't get my menstrual cycle or if it was abnormal, I wouldn't have known to say anything to her. I hated periods so I would have never said anything to her. With me having no clue how it all worked, I thought I was lucky not getting my cycle every month because I hated wearing those horrible pads. In hindsight, I realized if your menstrual cycle stopped or was weird, I needed to let someone know. It was way too late to learn that lesson now. A doctor at Parkland had just told us I was five months pregnant.

We pulled up to the house. Even though no one was home yet, I was afraid to get out the car. Eventually Mom would leave to get Dad and my siblings would return from school. I went straight to my room and got in the bed. I thought if I went to sleep before Dad got home I wouldn't have to talk to him until the next day. The nurse had given Mom something for me to start taking to help with the vomiting, as well as prenatal vitamins to start taking the next morning. I was in shock. Here I was fifteen, in the tenth grade, pregnant by a boy I didn't know. All of this because a girl I thought of as a childhood friend chose to set me up and take me somewhere I should have never been. I knew it was not a Christian thing to do, but I hated Genae. More than anyone in the world at that moment, I hated Genae for tricking me into the projects of West Dallas so she could be with her boyfriend. Genae, her boyfriend, and his friend were the cause of everything I was about to endure for the rest of my life. I was having a baby at age fifteen. I felt horrible and sick.

I lay in bed for a long time and eventually fell off to sleep. When I woke up, it was late in the evening and I could hear my siblings in other parts of the house. I knew if they were home, my dad was definitely in the house. I didn't want to leave my room for the night but I had to go to the restroom. I opened the door to my bedroom. Mom was in the kitchen. She asked me if I felt better. I told her I did. Physically, I was feeling a little better, but I was emotionally drained and distraught. I was pregnant.

I continued to the bathroom and tried staying in there as long as I could, fearful I would run into Dad on my way out. Someone knocked on the door forcing me to hurry. One of my siblings was waiting at the door.

They appeared to act normal, so that meant they didn't know anything about my bad news. Mom inquired if I was hungry. I told her no, but she insisted I eat something and told me to go to the dining table. As I entered the room, I could see Dad sitting in the living room. I wanted to run back into my room or better yet run directly out the front door. Where I was going to run off to was questionable. I took a seat and Mom gave me some soup and crackers then told me to eat so we could see if it stayed down. I ate and everything stayed down unlike the last few days. After I finished my meal, I got up and headed toward my room, but Dad called me to come see him. I thought I was going to be sick again as I could feel myself getting scared and nervous. I was embarrassed for my dad to look at me. What would he think? How would he treat me? Would I get a whooping or be put on punishment? Whether I wanted to or not, I had to face my daddy.

I turned to head in the direction of Dad. I thought for sure I would pass out from being nervous. I thought about throwing up so I could rush off to the bathroom and avoid him. Instead, I walked into the living room and stood. He was the only one in there. I prepared for Dad to yell and threaten me into telling him who I had sex with, when I had sex, where it happened and why I had not talk to them before now.

I was terrified of my dad's reaction. He told me to have a seat. Mom came into the room and took a seat as well. I hoped she could keep him from yelling too much or punishing me for what I did. My parents had no idea this was not my fault.

Dad started off by saying he was disappointed I was pregnant, however he was not mad or angry. He proceeded to tell me this type of thing happened and the best thing we could do as a family was stick together so we could all get through it. My dad had a very calm demeanor and told me he loved me and to hold my head up high because I was not the first young girl to get pregnant outside of marriage. Dad's calmness caught me off guard. I was speechless. I knew he had to be hurt by my actions. I looked over at Mom for confirmation to make sure she was hearing the same thing I was. The support in her expression told me everything was going to be okay. They said none of the other children knew so Dad was going to call a family meeting and tell my siblings the news.

Mom called my brother and sisters to the living room. Once they all got there, Dad told everyone he and Mom had something to tell them. I could see the curiosity in their faces as they looked at me strangely knowing I had already been talking with my parents about something. Dad stated the reason I had been so sick and might continue to be sick off and on was because I was pregnant. Someone said, "PREGNANT!" I was just as embarrassed sharing this horrible news with my siblings. Dad went on to tell them not to go around telling anyone what was going on. He and Mom would let people know when the time was right. All of their faces were in total shock, but I could tell they would be supportive just like Mom and Dad.

My siblings had lots of questions and our parents allowed them to speak. They wanted to know if this meant I was going to be a mother, if I was showing in my stomach, if I would continue to go to school. When would the baby be born? Would I still be allowed to participate in the church choir and our singing group? They had all kinds of questions and, to my surprise our parents answered each one of them. Then someone asked who was the daddy? Dad said we were not talking about any of that right now and not to ask about it again. I had told my parents before the family meeting it made me sad to talk about the boy and asked that they not make me tell them anything about him. They didn't know I didn't know him or that he had forced sex on me.

As crazy as it sounds, my parents never again asked who the boy was, where it happened or when it happened. They could do the math. I guess they figured it out based on the due date given at the clinic. All the other details I shut down about mentally and convinced myself I was not going to discuss it with anyone ever. Before Dad dismissed the family meeting, he told us there was nothing we could do about me being pregnant, however he was not going to raise grandbabies in this house. It was a warning to the other children not to think about having sex and coming home pregnant.

Now that Dad and my siblings knew, I felt a slight sense of relief. It was not a secret at least in my home and it was not to be broadcasted like an announcement to everyone. My parents decided we would deal with it on a need to know basis until it was obvious and then everyone would know. For now, everything would be family life as usual - school, church and home.

9

Three Months Carrying the *Sexual Assault/ Rape Baby* No One Ever Knew

Over the next month, nothing in our household changed drastically with the exception of me being six months pregnant and beginning to show. I was a tiny, petite girl at fifteen and did not gain much weight. No one could tell I was even pregnant. Mom pulled me out of school sports and the doctor said I was not allowed to participate in gym class either. She had to inform the school nurse of my situation to get me excused from those classes. A normal day consisted of me getting up to take my prenatal vitamins, going to school, coming home and doing my regular chores like my other siblings. I did have to sit down from the church choir, although I was able to continue with our family group rehearsals.

The horrible sickness I endured in the month of February had passed and instead of not being able to keep anything down, I ate or as Mom put it, craved everything. By the middle of my seventh month, I was showing. It seemed my stomach grew out of nowhere and almost everyone in my family, school, church and neighborhood knew I was pregnant. My extended family was very supportive. A couple of aunts on Mom's side of the family, Aunt Carolyn and Aunt Elyne, who I babysat for regularly and stayed the night with often, were extremely caring and shared lots of words of wisdom with me. My Aunt Carolyn could really relate since she already had children outside of marriage at a young age. She encouraged me to be strong and convinced me I was not the first or last girl to be pregnant in school.

Back then a fun thing for us to do with Mom, if we weren't at church or rehearsals, was to play outside with our cousins at my maternal grandparents' home. Since I was pregnant, I wasn't allowed to run around outside with the other siblings or cousins. On one of those special visits to my grandparents' house, my Aunt Carolyn asked me to take a walk so she could talk to me in private. As we walked, she encouraged me to stay in school, graduate with good grades and if I wanted to, plan on attending college. She wanted me to stay focused and not allow anyone to keep me from my dreams even though I was going to be a single mom. My aunt knew I dreamed of being a teacher so she encouraged me to keep that dream in view after I graduated high school. I loved her for those words.

After we had walked some distance, my aunt began to tell me about the first time she chose to have sex with her boyfriend. She said my grandparents nor anyone else knew they were meeting up to be together. Aunt Carolyn told me my grandparents didn't allow them to date without a sibling chaperone, so she and her boyfriend had to be sneaky. She asked if the baby's father was a secret boyfriend I didn't want my parents to know about. I told her I didn't have a boyfriend and didn't know anything about the father of the baby at all, not even his name. I could tell she didn't believe me because she looked at me like I was not telling the truth. I had never lied to my aunt so I was shocked when she looked at me like that. My aunt reminded me she and I had talked about a lot of things that were always kept between us. She said she wouldn't tell my mom or dad if I shared the name of the boy who got me pregnant. She promised it would stay between the two of us. I was sad that she really believed I had a secret boyfriend or that I knew the boy who got me pregnant. I had talked to my Aunt Carolyn more than my own mother about things, so for her not to believe me made me emotional. She reached over to rub my stomach. I began to cry and told her I was ready to go home. My aunt apologized for making me cry. Aunt Carolyn said she was only trying to help me talk about the baby's father to see if she could initiate a conversation between my parents and I. I told her I was never going to talk about what happened to me with anyone because I knew no one would believe me, especially now. My aunt hurt the inside of my heart that day. She would have been the only person next to my brother I could have told about that awful day in West Dallas. After our conversation, I knew I couldn't tell her either because I no longer trusted her to keep my secret. We walked back to my grandparents' house in silence.

After we made it back, I told Mom I was not feeling well and wanted to go home. I was upset and still crying. I saw my aunt step closer to my mom to talk with her. No doubt she was letting her know she had tried asking me about the father of the baby. My mom knew how close my aunt and I were. When I saw them talking, I figured it was partially her idea to put my aunt up to asking me about him. The idea of talking about what happened that day in October 1981 to my parents, my aunt or anyone for that matter was not something I was ever willing to do. It was bad enough knowing some boy forced me to have sex with him and impregnated me. I was hurt, sad, lost, confused, mentally drained, furious, and SUPER ashamed. I didn't want to talk about that day with anyone. I never planned to see that boy ever again in my life so what would be the point of bringing him up.

I thought as long as I had the help of my parents and family, I could take care of the baby by myself. How I was going to do that, I hadn't quite figured that part out.

The next morning I went to school late because it was time for my monthly appointment where they examined my stomach to so how big I had gotten. I had to visit the clinic every month so they could measure the baby's growth. I felt like everyone looking could tell I was pregnant because I had gained so much weight. At the appointment, the doctor told us the baby was growing well but had not turned correctly. He said there was still time for the baby to turn so there was no cause for alarm. I asked the nurse to explain what he meant. She said the baby had to position itself in time for him or her to come out correctly at birth. I still didn't understand what that meant. At fifteen, all this pregnancy and baby talk was way over my head. I was hoping Mom took it all in on my behalf and would explain things later.

It was close to the end of the school year, which meant summer break was quickly approaching. I was excited about being able to sleep in, however that summer would not be the same with me being pregnant. A baby was on the way and that would change everything. I was relieved that none of my friends, classmates or teachers treated me badly or made me feel horrible about being pregnant. To them, I was the same person and everyone expected me to return to school as a teenage mom after the summer break. The final weeks of school arrived and I passed my exams with no issues. When I returned to school in August, I would be entering my eleventh grade year as a mom. My siblings and I spent a lot of time over the summer break learning songs and rehearsing for the upcoming album. I felt like a normal teenage girl doing the same normal things I had done for years and I was glad my parents allowed that because it helped balance me out mentally. I recall Dad telling me on Sundays to stop holding my head down and walking around looking embarrassed when it was time to attend church. At home and school, I was myself. Being around the people at church had a different effect on me. I was always embarrassed and ashamed. My family support system was the greatest expression of love a girl in my position could have, even with them not knowing the story surrounding my pregnancy.

Early June, our group was having a huge rehearsal for the album. We had already recorded quite a few songs and our last night in the studio was going to be a long session. I was in my ninth month, which required weekly visits to the clinic that were exhausting. One morning while in the bathroom preparing for my appointment, I started to cough. I coughed so hard I wet my clothes a little. I ran to the toilet urinating like crazy with no end in sight. Mom called out for me to hurry so we wouldn't be late. I asked her to come to the bathroom door so I could tell her about my coughing and urinating.

Once she made it to the door, I told her what was going on with me. She asked to come in so she could check it out for herself. Mom looked at the water on the floor and told me my water broke and the baby was getting ready to come so we needed to go to the hospital instead of the clinic. I remember being afraid. I asked her to please let me sit until it stopped. Mom said I couldn't and that she was going to pick me out something else to wear and grab me a fresh pair of underwear. I took my time getting ready hoping the water would stop. It finally did. I slipped on the dress Mom gave me with the dry underwear and headed to the car. Mom paused to call Dad. As I walked down the steps, water trickled down my leg again. I told Mom I needed to go back to the bathroom and she forcefully said we had to get to the hospital now. Mom went inside the house and came back out with some large towels. I told her I didn't want to sit in Dad's Cadillac while I was still wetting myself. Mom became even more forceful in her tone and made me get in the car.

I sat there in birthing water as mom called it, mad. My dry clothes were wet and stuff ran down my legs. I felt yucky. Mom kept driving to the hospital. I remembered it was Wednesday, June 9th and became upset. It was our final night in the studio and I was going to miss it. Mom pulled the car up to the emergency room and told the medical staff I was fifteen years old, nine months pregnant and my water had broken. They came out with a wheelchair to put me in, wet clothes and all. I was so embarrassed. Mom went to park the car and finally joined me inside where they had already taken me to a room. Ready or not, the baby was on the way and all I could think about was missing our big studio recording.

10

He Look So Healthy, *How* Did That Happen and Can You Fix It?

I arrived at the hospital mid-morning, hungry. We had left home before I ate breakfast. They told me since the baby would be coming soon, I couldn't eat until after the birth, which made me upset. The doctor arrived to examine me and take some measurements. He had the nurses hook me up to a machine to monitor the baby's heartbeat which sounded loud and strong. I kept hearing them talk about my blood pressure going up and needing to get it down.

I was bored lying there waiting for something to happen and I could tell Mom was tired from having to sit there. Hours passed. Mom kept calling Dad to update him and my siblings, but there was no new information to pass along. I had not progressed any further after many hours nor was I having any contractions. The only thing Mom could tell Dad was that I was complaining about being hungry. I was starved. Mom had been sitting in the room with me the entire time. After a nurse told her it appeared we were in for a long evening, Mom decided to take a break and go downstairs. I thought maybe she was going to get some food and didn't want to upset me so she just told me she needed to walk around. I was exhausted from lying in the bed and eventually fell asleep.

By the time I woke up, Mom had returned and was in a corner of the room talking with the doctor and nurse. The nurse came over, disconnected the baby monitor and told me I needed to walk around the hospital. They helped me out of the bed and gave me another gown to put on in the correct direction so no one would see my backside. I helped Mom push my IV pole while we strolled up and down the hallways of Parkland, our local county hospital, trying to get the baby to move in the right direction. Mom repeatedly asked me if I felt any pain. I told her the same thing I told the doctor and nurses, the only pain I felt was my stomach growling from hunger. We walked around for a long time and then decided to head back to my room. It was perfect timing, as they were ready to hook me back up for the doctor to examine me again.

I wasn't experiencing any contractions, but the examinations from the doctor were painful enough. When night fell, my labor had not progressed any further so they decided to give me some medicine to increase the contractions. An hour after they did this, I experienced my first sign of pain. The doctor examined me again and told Mom the baby was still breech and they were going to try turning it around. The doctor and nurse began pushing on my stomach while reaching inside of me. I started crying. The baby was not cooperating with what they wanted it to do. They were concerned about my rising blood pressure and wanted to take action. Mom had a worried look on her face and kept talking to keep me calm.

The doctor was concerned about the possibility of a dry birth or serious complications because so much time had passed since my water broke. They needed to get the baby out quickly and safely. Dad called the room from the studio for an update. Mom said everyone was praying for me and waiting to see if it was a boy or a girl. The pain finally started getting worse. I felt like I was going to throw up so the nurse gave me a pan in case I got sick. Nothing came up. I was so dehydrated the doctor felt sorry for me and allowed me to have some ice chips. The ice tasted like a hamburger and french fries. Early the next morning, Mom called Dad to tell him there was still no baby and because my blood pressure continued to rise, they were going to take me into surgery to do an emergency C-section. I had never heard of a C-section. The doctor and nurse said since it had been over twenty hours and the baby was not turning, they would have to cut me open to get it out.

I began to cry. Mom asked me to calm down and said everything would be fine. After all that time lying there, walking around, getting medicine through the IV, this baby was not going to come naturally, as Mom called it. The baby's position inside my stomach forced me to have surgery. I hated that boy who had done this to me with everything I had inside my brain.

Mom asked me the weirdest question as they were preparing me for surgery. She wanted to know if I had any information so she could call the baby's father. I could tell from her facial expression and tone of voice she was upset about all I was going through. I wondered why she had asked me about the boy at that moment. I told Mom to hand me my purse. I reached inside and handed her the same piece of paper I had received from Genae in December. Before she could even ask, I told her that was all I had and I didn't know anything about him. I started crying harder wondering why I had kept that piece of paper all those months. The truth was I had no clue. As mad as I was at Genae that day, I had hidden the paper away in my purse instead of throwing it away. God had a reason for me holding on to it. I wondered if my mom would really call this Clint boy. I didn't even know if it was a real phone number. When Genae gave me that paper, I had no idea this boy's baby was already growing inside of me.

There was no turning back. I had given Mom the paper. Whatever she planned to do with it was on her. As the medical staff rushed in to prepare me for surgery, I felt terrified. The doctor told me he would join me in the operating room shortly. Mom spoke with Dad on the phone as the nurses prepped me. To this day, I have no idea if Dad made it to the hospital to be with Mom as she waited for me to come out of surgery with a baby.

More medical staff came in unplugging all kind of stuff and rolled me out of the room. Mom said she was praying for me, she loved me and that everything would be fine. She said she would be waiting for me after they got the baby out safely and told me not to worry about anything.

As they rolled me down the hall, I became frightened and cried out for my mom. In the operating room, the doctor told me they would put me to sleep so I wouldn't feel anything. He said when I woke up the baby would be out. They told me they were putting medicine in my. IV and I began to get sleepy staring at the lights on the ceiling. I could hear everything going on around me and felt tears running down my face. I heard the baby monitor; the heartbeat was still loud and strong. The nurses put cold stuff on my stomach and scrubbed really hard to clean it. I lay there thinking when I woke up I would be a mommy with a baby to take care of everyday. Slowly, everything began to fade and before you knew it, I was fast asleep.

The glimpse of sunlight told me it was morning. I wondered if I was out of surgery. The nurses were monitoring me because my blood pressure was elevated and wanted to know how I felt. I asked them what was going on and did I have the baby. One of them said I had a little boy. She said they were cleaning him up and would bring him to see me soon. Mom walked into the recovery room and said I had a handsome little boy.

Eventually, they brought in this precious baby boy who took over twenty hours to be born. He arrived on June 10, 1982, weighing five pounds and five ounces. I was scared and happy. I was now the mother of a cute little boy. He looked perfect to me, although I didn't get to see him long because they had to take him back to the nursery to feed him.

I had an extended stay in the recovery room due to overcrowding on the maternity ward. Parkland Hospital did not have a bed for me. Eventually, they rolled my hospital bed right into the center of a room with four other women and monitored my blood pressure from there. I looked really stupid lying in bed in the middle of the room.

The hospital had a system where they would bring the babies in the room to be with the mothers for their feedings. However, the nurses had informed Mom and I my son was being a little lazy with his feedings so they were watching him. Dad and my siblings brightened my day with a visit. Anxious to meet their new nephew, they had all stopped by the nursery to see him before coming to see me. Everyone said he was a cute, tiny, little boy. I was glad to see all of them and wanted to know how the studio session went for the album recording. Everyone was exhausted from the long night. After visiting with me for a little while, Dad was ready to leave to get some rest. Mom was very tired and left as well. They left me in the room by myself with the other moms and their babies. I was nervous about being away from home.

A nurse came to help me out of the bed the next day so I could take what they called a sitz-bath. I had never heard of that before, but it was actually refreshing after being in the same gown for over twenty-four hours. The nurse was kind. She not only bathed me but also took me for walks. After a woman checked out of the room later that day, the nurse moved me out of the middle of the floor and put me in one of the regular beds. Our meal and the babies arrived in the room almost at the same time.

I thought my baby boy was staying in the nursery so I kept eating since I was hungry, but a nurse brought my son to me. I was so happy. I stopped eating to take him in my arms. The bottle they gave me was different than the bottles the other women were using to feed their babies. The nurse said my baby was not sucking the other nipple well, so she had given me a "preemie" bottle, though I had no idea what that meant.

As she left the room, I started feeding him. He sucked the nipple for a second and then held it in his mouth. Another mom whose baby was not coming to the room that day came over to help me. She could see I was young and clueless. I let her hold my son so I could finish eating. I didn't realize that was against hospital policy until a nurse came in the room. She scolded me in a nice way advising me to never let anyone who was not a nurse in the hospital hold my baby. She saw that my baby boy whom I had not officially named was not feeding on the bottle for me either and told me she was going to take him back to the nursery.

After I ate, the nurse had me walk the halls to get things moving after my C-section. To be honest, with the exception of feeling the staples in my stomach, I didn't feel that bad. Once I completed my walk and was back in my bed, the nurse informed me a pediatric doctor would be coming to talk with me about why the baby was not taking the bottle. When the doctor entered the room, he pulled the curtain for privacy and asked me had I named the baby yet. I told him not officially, but I had settled on a name and would be giving that to the lady for his birth certificate. The doctor told me they had run some tests and was tube feeding my son. I didn't understand how any of that worked. I had no clue he was about to tell me my perfect looking baby boy conceived by force was born with two severe birth defects. This would crush my world for life.

The doctor said the baby was born with hydrocephalus and anencephaly. Of course, I did not understand what those words meant, but they sounded so terrible I knew it must be bad. The doctor used a pen and notepad to help me better understand what he was telling me. He drew a round circle in the shape of a head and started drawing lines that looked like waves of water. Then, he drew a short little object at the bottom of the circle. He continued telling me about the birth defects my son had, explaining that my son had an empty head. His head only had a brain stem or base, which was what the brain sat on and the rest of his head was full of water. Inside, there was no brain.

I wondered how my son would survive that way. How could he live without a brain? How did this happen? Where was my mom? Between the information the doctor was trying to tell me, and my own fearful questions, I lost it. I wanted my parents.

There was more information the doctor needed to share with me but I was sobbing uncontrollably and he could not get another word in. A nurse tried to console me and asked for a number to call my mom. I literally could not talk. I was an emotional wreck. They eventually looked it up in my charts because I remember them giving me the phone to talk to Mom. I tried telling her what they had just told me about the baby. She could tell I was extremely upset and said she was on her way back to the hospital. I had completely shut down so the doctor and nurse stopped trying to talk to me. No one knew my entire story as to how this baby was conceived not even my parents. So no one knew how overwhelming all of this was for me. I had just given birth to a little boy from a boy I knew nothing about and hated with everything in me. All because a mean girl name Genae tricked me into going to the projects of West Dallas and a selfish boy name Clint forced me to have sex with him. I was fifteen years old, faced with being not only the mother of a baby, but a baby with major medical issues. I felt God was punishing me and hated the fact I did not tell anyone from the beginning. In my mind, God was making me pay for my sin.

I couldn't wrap my head around what the doctor had said. The baby looked so normal and healthy. How did this happen to my son? Somewhere between the long labor and the horrible news the doctor delivered, "the baby" had become "my son." He was a part of me no matter how he got here. I was scared. I wondered if there was a way to fix the problem with an operation or something. Could birth defects like that be fixed? Could God fix it if I prayed for a miracle? God knew what happened to me. The devastating news I received on June 11, 1982, was nothing anyone could ever truly be prepared for.

At fifteen, I didn't know anything about sex. I didn't know what that boy did to me was considered rape or sexual assault, but God knew. He knew it was not my fault I had conceived a child by that boy. I cried out to God for help.

11

My Life and Home *Will* Never Be the Same Again

Mom arrived at the hospital, stopped by the nurses' station and told them she wanted to hear the information the doctor had conveyed to me. It was lunchtime when she arrived, but I had no appetite. The privacy drapes were still drawn around my bed when she entered the room. Not that the drapes offered any real privacy, all the other moms could hear most of what the doctor said and they could definitely hear me wailing. I continued to cry as Mom and I waited for the doctor. A nurse arrived to escort us to a conference room where the doctor would talk to us in private. I learned later the doctor had broken protocol when he did not do that earlier. Mom helped me get myself together as the nurse assisted me into a wheelchair. We headed to a conference room where the doctor and another lady were waiting.

As we entered the room, the doctor introduced himself to Mom and introduced the lady as a Parkland Hospital social worker who would help us make decisions and cope with everything they were telling us. The doctor asked Mom if I had informed her about the problems the baby was facing. In a calm, yet firm tone, Mom immediately told the doctor they should have called my parents prior to speaking to me about anything. She let the doctor and social worker know that I was fifteen and this type of information should have been told to me with my parents present. The doctor agreed and apologized.

The doctor shared that same drawing with Mom and explained to her the baby had two birth defects, hydrocephalus and anencephaly. He told us the first birth defect was very rare and when found in infants they referred to them as "water head babies." The second birth defect was also extremely rare and seldom heard of. They described it as an infant being born with a "premature brain" or "no brain" at all. My son was born with the brain stem only. I was still crying of course and Mom began to cry as well.

The social worker handed us tissue. The doctor allowed us a moment to compose ourselves and then informed us the baby's brain stem would only give him limited function, if any. He then went on to say as a result of the hydrocephalus and my son not having a brain, his life expectancy would be no greater than six months, if that. My world crashed under the weight of the doctor's devastating pronouncement.

I wasn't sure I understood completely so I asked the doctor what that meant. He reiterated that due to the severe birth defects, my son - the baby I knowingly carried inside of me the past four months would die about six months from the day of his birth. My thoughts were all over the place. I felt stupid. I was mad at myself for not telling anyone that boy had forced himself on me. I thought God was punishing the baby because I didn't fight back and I didn't tell my parents. All that time I had wasted protecting my secret and the baby was going to die. It no longer mattered to me if they knew the truth. Thinking all of these destructive thoughts, I cried even harder. The doctor told us with the baby being terminally ill and me being so young they were unsure if we should, could or wanted to take him home in that condition, thus the presence of the social worker at the meeting, to help me consider all of my options.

I was in utter disbelief. The social worker stated her name again and told us she was there to assist our family in whatever way she could. She had already been given the specifics on my case and had done some advanced research to help us out. She mentioned how difficult she knew this would be for me at such a young age and said there was a very nice institution in Houston, Texas, where my son could live and be taken care of until his death. I asked her how I would be able to see him and take care of him if they sent him to live in Houston since we lived in Dallas. She explained that we could visit him in the institution anytime we desired. I asked her if that meant they weren't going to allow me to take him home. Mom was quiet and fell into the routine we had become accustomed to since finding out I was pregnant. I was asked and expected to answer the questions. However, if I couldn't, she would speak up.

Anytime the doctor, nurses, or staff had anything to say, they directed their full attention to me since I was the patient. If I turned to Mom for more understanding she was allowed to jump in and help me answer questions or provide input.

I asked them why they were telling me about an institution and asked again if that meant they were not going to allow me to take my baby home the way he was. They said due to the severity of his birth defects and how rare they were, it would take a considerable amount of work and training to care for someone in his condition and that the staff in Houston was already equipped to take on his case. I felt like they were talking to me as if my son was a lost cause, like they were trying to do my family a favor by transferring him away from us until he died.

I was not happy with the way the conversation was going. My mom jumped in and said we would discuss it as a family and would not make any decisions at this time. Mom could clearly tell I was upset. The doctor told us they needed a decision in a couple of days and the social worker reinforced what he said. Due to the severity of my son's medical condition, he would no longer be allowed to visit in the room. They told me I would have to visit him in the Pediatric Intensive Care Unit (PICU) that was advanced enough to care for him until a decision was made.

Mom and I were silent as the nurse wheeled me back to the room. It felt like the same silence we had shared four months ago when the doctor told us I was pregnant, only this was a lot worse. Safely back in the room away from all the medical personnel, I broke down again. After Mom and I grieved for a bit, she called Dad to tell him everything that was going on. I heard her say, "See you soon," which meant Dad was on his way to the hospital. Someone came in to help me complete the birth certificate. I had not yet given my day old son a name. I had fallen in love with the letter J in school and enjoyed being creative so I made up a name for him. I named him Jaretton Jamal Thompson. Mom decided she was going to call him JJ or Tootie. Once Dad arrived at the hospital, he prayed for me, Jaretton, our family, the medical staff and everyone involved in the baby's life. Dad nicknamed him Vadimir. Though I never knew what that meant at the time, I later discovered it meant peace.

Mom mentioned she had called the number on the piece of paper I gave her the day before. She said she had asked to speak to Clint, but he was not home. She briefly spoke to his mother and told her who she was. Mom told the lady where we lived and that she had a fifteen year old daughter who had just given birth to a baby boy and I had given her a piece of paper with Clint's name and phone number on it. She told his mom I had informed her Clint was the boy who got me pregnant. Mom wanted Clint to know about the baby. She said his mother was nice and would call her back after speaking to her son, which she did. Clint told his mother he didn't know Valarie Thompson or anything about a girl from North Park being pregnant by him. Mom thanked the lady for calling back and that was the end of that. Clint was partially correct when he told his mother he didn't know me, though he failed to confess he'd forced me, a girl he didn't know, to have sex with him at their home in October as I lay crying and begging him to stop. I guess he didn't want her to know he, Genae and his friend set me up. My parents still didn't know what happened to me. After hearing he lied to his mother, I remained convinced keeping the details of that day between me and God was the right thing to do.

My parents and I went to see Jaretton in the nursery. He looked so normal it was hard to believe he had such rare and unusual birth defects. His little body was perfect. He was adorable. Lying in an incubator in PICU, he had a little cap on his head. I wasn't sure why he was in the incubator so I asked the nurse. They said it was to help regulate his body temperature. Even though he was not sucking on a bottle very well, the nurses allowed me to feed him with the preemie bottle. After seeing he wasn't latching on, they told us he would be fed intravenously throughout the night. Most of what they said went over my head. I was too young to comprehend it all. After the visit, we headed back up to my room.

I knew Dad and Mom had talked while I was visiting Jaretton inside the special nursery because Dad wanted to know how I felt about everything. I told him I understood the baby was very sick and would die in a few months, but I really wanted to take him home. I didn't want him to live in an institution in Houston cared for by strangers none of us knew. It was not like he knew me either since he was just a baby and all, I just thought since I was his mother it was my responsibility to care for him. I told Dad no matter how long he lived I wanted him to be at home with us. Our family bond was strong. My parents had always been very supportive of my siblings and me. I only had to say it one time. Dad spoke up and said if I wanted to take him home then that was exactly what I could do. I cried tears of joy. I was the happiest girl ever and thanked Dad for giving me permission to bring my baby home. Mom told me when the doctor came to visit the next morning I was to tell him we had made a decision. However, it would be discussed in person once she made it to the hospital. Once again, a decision I made changed my life forever.

12

Caring for My *Terminally* Ill Miracle Baby Boy

On June 12, 1982, Mom arrived early so we could inform the doctor of my decision. She was prepared to stand by my side and hear everything they would tell me. I got up that morning to take my sitz bath, eat breakfast and walk the halls like they required of me after having a C-section. I was getting regular shots in my hip throughout the day because my blood pressure remained elevated. I was anxious to tell them our decision so I could go to PICU and hold my baby. The doctor finally came to see me. Instead of taking me to the conference room, he closed the privacy curtains around my bed. The nursing staff had already informed him I had made a decision regarding the baby. Mom looked at me as if to say go ahead, speak up. I guess she was preparing me to be the parent and make the decisions regarding my son and his future.

I asked the doctor why he believed my son would only live six months. He explained since the baby had no brain he wouldn't know how to do normal things like suck a bottle, regulate his own body temperature, cry to let us know something was wrong, etc. He said his brain stem would only assist in some simple reflex functions. I was beginning to understand and knew I would have to learn more as time went on. I told the doctor after discussing everything with my parents and receiving their blessing and promise of support, I was going to take the baby home and care for him as long as God allowed him to live. I didn't have the heart to send my son away to an institution for him to die alone without being there to care for him.

The doctor smiled and said he thought that would be my decision based on my emotional response during our initial conversation. He said he felt the love coming from me so he was not at all surprised. It was settled. The doctor said the social worker would come by to talk with me as we had a lot of things to go over in preparation for us to go home. He also told us the pediatric nurses would teach me how to tube feed the baby and everything else I needed to know to care for him in our home. He called me a strong determined teenage girl and he wished me the best.

I was ready to learn. I had been praying daily, but it felt like I should start praying much harder for a miracle once JJ was in my care. I understood what the doctor said, but I was raised to trust God and believe in miracles. From an early age, I was brought up in church where we were taught God had the final say about everything in life. Even when the doctors told you one thing, it didn't mean God could not change the outcome. If ever there was a time to lean on God and be stronger in my faith, the decision to take JJ home was that moment.

The baby and I were in the hospital for three weeks. I had my own health issues the doctors were concerned about. My blood pressure continued to be elevated and they were also trying to help me gain weight. The doctor thought I needed to be at least one hundred pounds before he released me. I was okay being in the hospital because Jaretton could not be released until I satisfied their requirement that I learn everything I needed to know to care for him on my own. During this time, the nurses taught me how to guide the feeding tube into the middle of his stomach. I had to insert it gently through his nostril, and then take a syringe and suction the fluid from his stomach. This was to insure the tube was properly inserted before giving him a special formula made from starch that provided certain nutrients he needed per the pediatric doctor's instructions. There was so much for me to learn but my determination and willpower never waivered.

I had to take CPR classes so I would know how to resuscitate JJ if he failed to take a breath. I also had to take his temperature constantly to make sure it was at least 98.6 degrees. I was enrolled in medical classes that were specific to my son's care. I also attended meetings facilitated by the social worker for emotional support to aid my preparation in caring for a terminally ill child. My entire life changed for this little baby boy.

Everyone at Parkland County Hospital was so impressed by what I was doing at my age. I was a few weeks shy of sixteen and all I wanted for my birthday was to take my son home. My blood pressure finally returned to normal and my weight was up to ninety-eight pounds. The doctor was pleased and said I would be going home soon. The thought of taking JJ home and sleeping in my own bed excited me.

I completed my final day of classes and the pediatric staff gave the doctor a glowing report on all I had accomplished while learning the specialized techniques required to care for JJ. My primary doctor was also happy with my physical condition after having an emergency C-section. He completed his exam and said although my weight was not at the one hundred pound mark, everything else was good and he would be releasing me from the hospital. I would finally get to go home with Jaretton. I was overjoyed, until the doctor told me his release was only for me and that the pediatric doctor was in control of releasing my son from PICU.

I called Mom to tell her the good news about being released so she could prepare to pick us up. It took her a couple of hours to get to the hospital but her timing could not have been more perfect. The pediatric doctor wanted to talk with us about releasing JJ. I followed the pediatric doctor to the nursery thinking I was going to pick up my son. However, when we arrived in PICU, the doctor said he would not be able to release JJ until there was an incubator assigned to us for our home. They were uncomfortable because his body was not stabilizing a normal temperature of 98.6 outside the incubator so they agreed it was best to have one in our home. The social worker assigned to my case had not been able to find the type of incubator we needed and until they did, JJ would have to stay at the hospital in the Pediatric Intensive Care Unit. I blurted out did this mean he couldn't come home with me. They confirmed he would have to stay until an incubator was secured.

I was crying uncontrollably and asked if I could please check back in so I could stay there with him. They told me that was impossible because there was no medical reason to keep me there. I looked at Mom but there was nothing she could do. The doctor and nurses said I was allowed to visit him every day to feed him, bathe him and do all the other things I had learned until he was able to come home. I wondered why they thought that would make me happy. I was sad and nothing changed that. I had checked out and would have to leave JJ at the hospital until a large incubator was found for us to rent. Mom took me home. I walked to the car with my head down, sobbing. I crawled into the backseat and started to lay down when Mom reminded me of the C-section. Mom tried to comfort me with tender words. I did not have the heart to respond so she gave up. Dad and my siblings welcomed us home with a sign for me and JJ. Mom let them know JJ would not be coming home right away. I went to my room and sat on the bed. One by one, my siblings knocked on my door and asked if they could come in to talk to me. I turned everyone away. Eventually, they all got the picture. I was not in a good mood. My mind was going crazy. Questions to God flooded my heart. God, why are you being so mean to me? God, how long are you going to punish me and JJ? God, do you want my son to die at the hospital without his mom? I was exhausted and immediately fell into a state of depression. I cried out to God to fix this. Though I was questioning God, I knew He was the only one who could make this all better for me. I needed a miracle to come quick before I lost my mind. I went to sleep so I could wake up to go see JJ.

The next morning I got up early. I had already told Mom I wanted to be at the hospital as soon as the pediatric nursery allowed me to be there. She was supportive and ready to help me do whatever I needed to do for my son. Right before we walked out the door, the social worker called to inform us there was still no luck finding an incubator to rent, but she had good news. I wondered what kind of good news she could possibly have if there was no incubator for JJ to come home. She said the entire hospital was so proud of my desire and drive to take my son home and care for him that they decided to allow me to use one of their large incubators free of charge as long as he needed it. I screamed out loud and my mom and siblings ran into the room to see if I was crying or laughing. The social worker said they would be delivering the incubator and setting it up within the next hour or two so I needed to be at home. I was overwhelmed with joy. I asked her if that meant I could bring JJ home and she said yes. God had heard my cry.

JJ's homecoming was the best early sixteenth birthday present ever. My entire family was happy for me. I was ready to watch God work a miracle in my baby. The delivery of the incubator came just as promised and Mom and I left to go get my precious son. I was excited and nervous.

I remember the day like it was yesterday. It felt surreal. My son was finally checking out of Children's Medical Center of Dallas. The pediatric nursery staff was teary eyed as they packed up all JJ's items. The nurses gave us extra little cap warmers someone had made especially for his head, extra supplies of the ingredients needed to make his special formula, diapers on top of diapers on top of diapers, syringes, feeding tubes and everything else they had used in his daily care. They were all happy to see me take him home and sad to see him go because they had gotten attached to him. It was the best feeling ever to place my baby boy in his car seat inside my parents' car and take him home.

Over the next two months, I developed a routine for caring for JJ. I knew how to make the formula, insert and eject his feeding tube, and monitor his temperature and breathing. My Mom was my biggest supporter. She learned everything I did so she would be able to help me care for him.

Summer break ended quickly and I returned to school as an eleventh grader. I was excited to be a junior in high school and very afraid to leave the house without taking JJ anywhere I went. Since Mom was already a stay at home mother, she agreed to babysit for me during the day while I attended school. She also allowed me to continue my extracurricular activities, like sports. I adjusted my morning routine so I could take care of JJ before I dressed and left to catch the school bus. I was appreciative of Mom, but didn't want to take advantage of her kindness.

In those first few months of his life, JJ quickly became my world. I was an ordinary sixteen year old who enjoyed school, church and friends, however my priorities shifted once I became a mommy. I was in it all the way. When Mom and I disagreed about how things should be done, I had to remind her I was JJ's mother. Although I appreciated her help and suggestions, the final decisions regarding him were up to me. I remained open to her advice and at times shifted in her direction, however I was in love with my little boy and his care was 100% mine.

I was consumed with keeping up with my studies and rushing home every day to relieve Mom of my son so I could take him to my room and care for all his needs. I did this every day for the next six months and every day it was agonizing to think any day I could get a call or come home to discover my son was dead. I continued to attend counseling for parents with terminally ill children.

Guys from North and West Dallas often teased me, calling me "square" and preacher's daughter, but there were a few guys from West Dallas I became close friends with. I met them all in junior high when they were bussed to our schools in North Dallas. They were like "pretend" big brothers. I confided in one guy name Gregory, we called him Pop. In a sense, he took being one of my "play" big brothers at school for real. I couldn't talk to my own parents about what happened, but I knew my friend Pop would believe me once I told him what transpired. Coincidentally, Pop lived in the projects close to Clint. He told me Clint was nineteen and out of high school. Pop was shocked to learn Clint was the guy who tricked me into being at his house and got me pregnant. When I told him Clint lied to his mother and said he knew nothing about me, Pop was upset.

Unbeknownst to me, this was actually something that happened to girls back in the day. It was some sort of game for boys to go after virgin girls and try to get them to have sex, albeit not through machination. Pop felt bad for me. He was going to make Clint admit he knew me and then see my son face to face. I told Pop I didn't want anything from Clint nor did I want any trouble. My parents could never find out. He convinced me to let him handle it. Pop set it up where he and two other guys we knew from school tricked Clint into thinking they had a girl in North Dallas for him to meet. My family was at bible class one evening and JJ and I were home alone. There was a knock on the door. Pop and the other guys walked into the house toward the den area where JJ and I were. Clint was directly behind them. I will never forget the look on his face as he stumbled to say hello.

Pop asked Clint if he remembered me coming to the projects with a girl name Genae. Clint admitted he did. Pop then asked him if he also knew he had gotten me pregnant when he had sex with me last year. Clint told Pop he remembered his mom getting a phone call from a lady saying her daughter had given birth to a baby boy and he was the father. Embarrassed, Clint looked at me.

I was nervous, but for the first time since that day in October, I spoke up. I told him because he'd forced me to have sex, the baby boy lying on the couch was his. He looked at JJ in disbelief, focusing on the tube and his nostril tape. I explained he was born very sick and gave no further details as I started to get emotional. My friend Pop was satisfied bringing him over so I could confront him and they left before my parents got home from church. That was the last time I saw Clint and the only time he ever saw JJ.

One evening, when JJ was seven months old, he had to be rushed to the emergency room. He was having a hard time trying to catch his breath and his body was jerking. Tests revealed there was a lot of water built up inside his head causing him to have seizures and shallow breaths. Everyone was impressed by the love and level of care he was receiving at home, yet surprised he was still alive with all the problems he had endured. JJ was scheduled for emergency surgery to place a shunt inside his head that would drain the water from his head into his stomach and alleviate the built up pressure. We honestly hadn't noticed how enlarged his head had become until it was pointed out to us by a physician in the emergency room. In those seven months, no one that came in contact with JJ on a regular basis had noticed his head growth, not family members, the clinical staff, the home therapist, or social worker, and JJ had frequent appointments with a pediatric specialist because of his drastic birth defects. It was a mystery to all of us how something so drastic went unnoticed, but the excess fluid buildup caused his head to stretch in width and length. This could not be reversed, but the shunt helped with releasing the water, thus preventing his head from growing any larger. The surgery went well. JJ stayed in the hospital about a week before he returned home.

My back-up sitter, Aunt Carolyn, only lived one block from our house. She was attached to JJ and kept him on several occasions whenever Mom needed to run errands without taking him along. One evening while Mom was in Houston attending a women's conference, I picked JJ up from my aunt's home and noticed he was sleeping a lot and not acting like his normal self. I called my aunt to see if she had observed anything abnormal while he was with her. She said he had done the same with her and told me to keep an eye on him and let her know if I needed anything.

As the night went on, JJ's temperature fell and nothing I tried returned it to normal. He had only used the incubator for three months before he outgrew it. I had to keep the room within a good temperature range and monitor his body manually. When his breathing turned shallow, I became nervous and had my dad drop us off at Parkland Hospital. As a terminally ill baby, JJ had high priority in the emergency room and we were seen right away.

Once we were checked in, they discovered he had an infection in his shunt. I called to let Dad know they were going to admit him and start an IV to give him antibiotics. Dad said he would call Mom. He also called my Aunt Carolyn because she called the hospital to see if I wanted her to come stay with me. I told her we would be okay and settled in to our home away from home. They plugged JJ up to an IV and a monitor for his breathing. After everything calmed down, I pulled out the faithful hospital bed they stored in the room for parents who wanted to stay overnight and fell asleep. I was sleeping very well until I heard a loud noise.

Doctors and nurses ran like crazy into JJ's room, startling me. I then realized the noise was the alarm on JJ's breathing monitor. I jumped up and asked what happened. The nurses informed me his breathing had totally stopped and asked me to leave the room. I was scared to death and began to cry. A nurse came to comfort me saying they would do everything possible for him. I heard them calling code blue but didn't know what that meant. She asked if there was anyone she could call for me. I asked her to call my dad since Mom was out of town. They worked on JJ and it seemed like hours passed before my dad and my brother arrived.

The doctor finally walked out of JJ's room and asked us to follow him. He led us to the conference room. I asked if JJ was dead. The doctor told me he was not. I asked to go see him because I needed to see my son's face and he said I could after he informed me about what happened. The severe birth defects and the infection in JJ's shunt had caused his body temperature to fall drastically. When his breathing stopped, they took every measure to revive him. Even though they were successful, they were unsure if he would make it through the night based on how long it took for him to come back around. My dad and brother tried to console me, but I cried uncontrollably. The doctors said there was nothing more we could do except wait. Dad asked if we could go see JJ. When I opened the door to his room, JJ lay there looking lifeless. In addition to his feeding tube, he was hooked up to several more tubes. I stood there crying softly, watching his chest go up and down. Dad immediately began to pray out loud asking

God to touch JJ's body and to give me strength. I knew Dad couldn't stay at the hospital because he had to work and get the other siblings off to school with Mom being out of town. My brother offered to come back and stay with me, but I told them both I was not afraid to stay by myself and that I would be okay alone. Before they left, Dad called Mom in Houston. Talking to her made me feel better. Mom offered to come home early, however God had given me peace in my heart. I told her I would be okay and I would call Aunt Carolyn if I needed someone to be with me until she returned.

JJ made it through the night without any more episodes of not breathing and my brother came to stay with me during the day to keep me company. After alerting the nurses, I left JJ's room and walked to the cafeteria. My brother and I were enjoying our conversation when a page sounded over the loud speaker calling for Valarie Thompson to come back to the floor. My heart dropped. I thought not again. When we arrived on the floor, doctors and nurses were coming out of JJ's room. Once again I was taken to the conference room with my brother who was my adult that day. I thought for certain my baby boy was dead. My eyes welled with tears as the doctor informed us JJ had another episode where he stopped breathing and was revived. My son was fighting for his life and the idea of him being resuscitated a second time in less than twenty-four hours was very bad news.

The doctor told me I needed to make a decision about JJ's care. Since my son had already stopped breathing twice in such a short time, I had to sign a medical document that basically gave the hospital consent to revive him by any means necessary. I didn't understand what the doctor was requiring of me so I asked for clarification. He further explained my son's little body had been brought back to life twice in such a short time it would be too much for his heart to try a third time without the risk of complications. If JJ was not able to start breathing on his own, they would hook him up to a breathing machine that he would most likely be forced to stay on until his death. If that happened, JJ would never be able to go home again. Inside my head I screamed, NO WAY. I had to decide whether or not my son died. I desperately needed my mom.

There was no way for me to wait until Mom returned. As Jaretton's mom, they were asking me to make a quick decision and sign off on it. I asked for a few minutes to call my mom. Mom wanted to know if we could wait and have the discussion when she came back home. My brother and I told her the doctors weren't willing to take that chance since JJ had already coded twice. Mom told me I had to decide and she supported whatever I chose to do. I was sixteen years old. I didn't know what to do. I wondered why God was doing this to me.

The nurses went to retrieve the paperwork I would be required to sign, giving my brother and I a private moment to talk. My brother was nineteen, only three years older than I, but he said something I would never forget. My big brother said, "Little sister, you have to rely on your faith in God and go with that decision. It will be the right one." I was praying hard to God for guidance and once my brother said those words, I knew in my heart I would make the right choice.

When the doctor and nurses came back, I took the papers and held them. They showed me what each section meant and where my initials went. I felt the presence of God directing me the entire time. I was ready to finalize my decision in writing with my brother co-signing as my adult guardian. I initialed the places that stated something like if the patient were to stop breathing I give up the rights for them to resuscitate him. This clearly meant when or if JJ stopped breathing again, I wouldn't want him to be hooked up to a breathing machine to live out the remainder of his life in that manner.

I told my brother if God was ready to take my son away from me, I would not be selfish hooking him up to a machine until he died just to keep him with me. I never wanted him in an institution and I felt in my heart if a machine was breathing for him that was no better than letting them take him to Houston to die. I initialed everywhere I was told and signed the document with my brother there to support my decision. There was no turning back now.

That next day, JJ's breathing stabilized and the medication was clearing up the infection inside his shunt. With everything that had gone on the past two days, all he could do was sleep. That afternoon, my mom arrived back in town and immediately came to the hospital to check on us. JJ opened his eyes, which was incredible. He had not done that since arriving in the emergency room. Mom joked that he was just waiting on his granny to get back because he missed her so much. I smiled and returned the joke saying that was why he stopped breathing twice, to get her back home. Then I told her I was glad she was back as well. JJ continued to progress and never had any more episodes of not breathing during that hospital stay. Once the infection cleared and JJ was taking his feedings by tube, we were able to go home. I never thanked God so much in my life before. My son was truly a miracle baby. That little boy was beating all the odds. No matter what additional challenges lay ahead, I felt like we were up for the fight.

13

God After All I Did, *Why* Didn't You Do Your Part For Me?

As a sixteen-year-old teenage mom of a terminally ill baby boy, our struggle was real but JJ had a lot more living to do and I had a lot more parenting to do. After going through that horrible experience, I didn't think things could get any worse. I understood what the doctors told me about JJ's life expectancy, but we had already surpassed that.

My school term was about to end and summer would begin. Even with everything going on with JJ, I managed to go to school every day and keep up. I only missed class one time when JJ was hospitalized and Mom was out of town. I continued to play volleyball, basketball and assisted on the track team, along with taking care of my son everyday. I was one proud young mother. Taking care of JJ was my entire world; nothing else mattered. That summer break would be super special. JJ's first birthday was June 10, 1983, and I threw him the biggest party ever.

My son beat the odds and lived to see his first birthday. All of his cousins, friends from the neighborhood, and church were there to help us celebrate the grand occasion. My Aunt Carolyn helped me plan the event and opened her home for JJ's party. A week or so before the party, JJ became ill and had to be hospitalized. I was concerned we would have to cancel the party, but he was released. I purchased the cutest outfit, complete with new shoes with bells so he could make some noise and we all had a fun time celebrating him.

Over the next few months, JJ had great days and not so great days. We had many more hospital stays and infections inside his shunt. One of the hardest things to watch him experience were those awful seizures. His entire body tensed and he would cry out in pain. There was nothing I could do for him. Sometimes, I rubbed his head and cradled his little body, rocking him gently. That seemed to ease the pain and abate the seizures. Then there were those days when nothing worked and they lasted for over an hour at a time. The doctor had prescribed a seizure medication, but over time, his body became immune and the drug no longer worked as effectively as it once did.

By the time the second winter rolled around, Mom and I were very experienced with dressing JJ appropriately to make sure his body temperature was always at 98.6. With the weekly home therapy visits and the monthly doctor visits, I had become a pro at taking care of his needs. Not only could I do routine things like tube feed him and monitor his temperature, I also knew how to perform CPR when his breathing was off, do physical therapy to keep his joints from becoming stiff, apply special back pats to allay the seizures and so much more.

With the exception of school, my little boy went everywhere I went. Mom brought him to some of my volleyball games. I took him to church and strolled him up and down the sidewalk so he could experience the outdoors and get fresh air like other kids his age. I carried him to every family function we had and took him to the amusement park.

On JJ's first trip to Six Flags, Mom and I sat waiting for my siblings with JJ in his stroller. A man who was operating one of the games walked over to take a closer look at him. The attendant observed my son's obvious birth defect with his enlarged head and asked if he could give him something. The kind gentleman walked away and came back with a large stuffed animal.

We were use to people staring at the shape of JJ's large head and little petite body. Some asked questions and I graciously explained about his condition. Others shook their heads, which annoyed me. I preferred people to ask rather than walk away like he was a freak or something.

During my final year of high school, I decided I would attend college in the fall and take JJ with me. Mom was happy about me going to college. She was not happy that I was taking JJ with me. We had several fallouts about JJ and I had to remind her he was my child and whatever decisions I made for him, she would have to accept even if she didn't like it.

I appreciated everything my mom did and never took anything for granted. She was JJ's secondary caretaker, however he was ultimately my responsibility and I never wanted her to think differently. I had observed other teenage girls who became teen moms in my family and in the neighborhood whose mothers were actually raising their children. I did not want to be that girl. JJ was not going to end up being raised by my mother. I had promised God and myself that I would raise and care for my child no matter what.

I had dreamed of being a teacher for as long as I could remember, but being forced to be a teenage mom of a special needs child altered my dream. If all went well, JJ and I would be attending Texas Woman's University where I would pursue a degree as a registered nurse. Because of my experience with JJ, my heart was set on being a pediatric nurse working with sick babies. I worked with a counselor and a special needs social worker to get our apartment set up in Denton, Texas. I was scheduled to graduate a few months early. After finalizing a few tasks, I would transition into college life.

Graduation day came so fast; I was anxious to walk across the stage. The last two years had been challenging and difficult. One fall day had changed the course of my life. I'd left home to attend the State Fair parade, ended up tricked by a childhood friend, forced to engage in sexual activity, only to find out five months later I was pregnant. I had endured a long labor and ended up with a terminally ill baby all at the tender age of fifteen. Somehow, I had survived. Not only had I made it, JJ had as well. Two weeks after my graduation day, JJ turned two years old.

On graduation day, I was allowed to hang out overnight to celebrate. It was the first and only time I had ever been away overnight from my son since his birth on June 10, 1982. I enjoyed my night out and had the best time with my friends. However the next day, I was back taking care of JJ. On June 10, 1984, we celebrated JJ's second birthday at our house. I readied JJ and I to leave for college in late August, throwing away items he and I no longer used to make sure I was only taking things we needed. To prepare him for living alone with me in Denton, JJ attended a local daycare a few hours each day.

I felt blessed by the support of my family, the hospital, the social workers and everyone in and outside of our circle. On July 15, 1984, I turned eighteen years old. Early August arrived and JJ was not feeling well so we rushed him to the emergency room. His seizures had worsened, lasting hours at a time, back to back. He had also spiked an extremely high fever and the medication that normally brought his temperature down was not working. Everyone was concerned. The doctors decided to admit him to the Children's Medical Center of Dallas. The place had become our second home over the past two years. I had Mom pack me a bag and prayed JJ would get better quickly so we didn't have to be there too long.

It turned out we were there a couple of weeks. JJ's fever was uncontrollably high. They could only bring it down with cold baths. They gave him higher doses of Phenobarbital in order to limit the frequency of his seizures. JJ was sleeping more than he had ever slept in his life. No one thought he would be going home anytime soon. The social worker made a couple of visits to the hospital to discuss the improbability of me taking

JJ to Denton alone. She said whenever he was feeling better and ready to be released from the hospital, I could have my mom bring him to me. That was not an option for me. I had never left my son's side except graduation night and I was not going to with him being so sick.

The doctors were able to stabilize the seizures and bring JJ's fever down. For weeks, all JJ did was sleep all day. In our normal daily routine, we alternated tube feeding and bottle-feeding. During this hospital stay, JJ would not wake up to take a bottle so I knew he was not feeling well. He never stopped breathing, which was comforting. Even though the paperwork remained in place if he stopped breathing, I did not want to think about that scary hospital stay from when he was seven months old. The thought of my baby being hooked up to a life support machine to breathe was never going to be my choice for him, not even after he had been with me for two years. I had made that decision at sixteen and I never changed my mind.

JJ's lengthy hospital stay prior to us leaving Dallas caused me to reconsider my plans for college, at least for the first semester. As I had been doing from the day he was born, I prayed everyday that God would miraculously heal his body. I had spent the past two years caring for my son's every need. I loved him with all of my heart. Mom tried unsuccessfully to get me to leave his bedside, but there was no reason for me to leave. He was in a private room and I had my own bed and bathroom. I didn't want to miss one precious moment with him.

One Sunday, JJ had a very rough night. His seizures were back to back. I hardly slept that night as the nurses were in there checking on him like clockwork. The next morning, I called Mom to tell her about JJ's night. She told me she would come sit with him so I could take a nap. Being at JJ's bedside consumed me. The only time I left was to go to the cafeteria for food.

I will never forget the day. Monday, August 20, 1984. Mom arrived at the hospital that morning. I had asked her to bring me more clothes. When she opened the door, I asked for my bag so I could shower and freshen up. I am not certain if she did it on purpose or if she honestly forgot, but Mom said she forgot to pack me a bag and she would take me home to shower and repack more things for myself. I was upset because she knew I had no intention of ever leaving JJ alone for any length of time. I had a huge attitude and started to pout because I needed undergarments and clothes really bad. Mom reiterated that she would run me to the house to get what I needed and I could bathe there.

I told Mom I really didn't want to leave JJ, but I needed to get some things for a few more days. She said it would do me good to get out for about an hour and if we left right then, she would bring me back after I took a bath and grabbed more clothing, reminding me that I had not left the hospital in weeks.

I relented. I changed JJ's diaper to make sure he was comfortable before I left. His hospital room was decorated with the coolest helium balloons. As I walked out the door, I remember saying I needed to take them down when I returned. They were almost on the floor so it was definitely time to brighten up the room with new ones.

I made sure to stop by the desk and let JJ's nurses know I was going home for a little while and would be back as soon as possible. The nurses were happy Mom finally got me to leave the hospital. They assured me they would watch JJ closely until I made it back to care for him.

Everyone, except me, thought it was a grand idea that I left the hospital and gave myself a break. I had literally been in the hospital room with JJ since his emergency admission. My siblings were shocked to see me when we arrived home. While I was glad to see them, I moved quickly. I wanted to bathe, pack and get back to the hospital. It was almost eleven when I told Mom I was ready to head back to the hospital.

Mom parked the car and we headed toward JJ's room. In my haste, we had not eaten and Mom insisted we stop in the café to eat. I told her she could but I needed to get back to JJ. Mom said she would bring me something and I said okay and headed to the elevator. I reached JJ's floor, exited the elevator and walked toward his room. I could see a lot of people standing in the hallway near the location of his room. The more I walked toward his room, the sicker I felt in my stomach. Why were they standing out there? What were they doing? Did something happen?

The closer I got, I could see JJ's doctor and several of his nurses. Something was wrong. Oh my, God, I thought, please let my baby be okay. I ran toward his room. When I reached the door, I heard someone say they were sorry. I wondered who they were talking to and rushed passed them. I needed to get to JJ.

As I entered his room, the first thing I noticed was the helium balloons. They had sunk to the floor. I burst into tears. The balloons were hanging in mid-air when I left for that short trip home and now they were touching the floor. Somehow in that moment, I equated the balloons being on the ground to the death of my son. I rushed closer to JJ's bed and let out a loud scream.

My baby was lifeless. Several of his tubes had been pulled out and were lying around the bed. The machine that monitored his heartbeat and vital signs was silent. I demanded the doctors tell me what happened. I picked JJ up, pleading with him to wake up, begging him not to leave me. I was screaming so loud. I started asking for my mom. They asked me if I needed to call someone. In my delirium, I was able to tell them my mom was downstairs getting food. I held my baby boy. A nurse brought over a chair and asked me to sit. She told me I could hold him as long as I needed. I rocked JJ gently and begged him to wake up. I was in shock, waves of helplessness washed over me. How was it possible that my son, Jaretton Jamal Thompson, was dead in my arms? I was no longer the only person crying out loud. I heard Mom crying, telling me she was so sorry.

I felt like my life had ended. How could God fail me after I prayed and prayed? I had promised Him I would be the best teenage mother ever even though He had given me a terminally ill baby. How many times had I cried out for a miracle? Why did God do this to me? I was sad, angry, confused, hurt and exhausted in my mind, body and spirit. All I had done for my son. I thought maybe God did hate me for what He allowed to happen with that boy and then me choosing not to tell my parents. I felt like God would punish me forever for not sharing my secret with anyone.

My entire body was numb. All I could do was cry and rock my baby boy back and forth hoping he would surprise us all and wake up. I heard Mom on the phone telling Dad Valarie's baby had passed away. Dad assured her the family was on their way to the hospital. The hospital chaplain came in and asked if he could pray with us. Mom told him that would be fine. He asked something else and Mom told him my dad was a pastor and was in route to be with us.

Mom wanted to hold JJ, which I allowed her to do. I began walking around his room. I couldn't figure out what I was supposed to do now. I had spent the last two years caring for my son. On a table next to his hospital crib was a notepad from one of the doctors with the words "time of death." As I looked at the clock on the wall, I realized JJ had only died a short time before Mom and I made it back to the hospital. I was sick.

In a fit of anger, I told Mom I had never wanted to leave and go home. I was not thinking or trying to hurt her feelings. I knew she felt horrible for making me leave. It was never my intention to make her feel worse.

I was bothered in my spirit at the thought of leaving JJ alone. I was wracked with guilt for not holding my ground and staying with him. None of that mattered. My son was dead. I gathered him from my mom and noticed his diaper was wet. I complained that even though he was dead they should still change his diaper. Sobbing, I laid him in the crib and reached for a diaper and wipes to clean him up. When I picked him back up, JJ gave a hard sigh. The doctors had forewarned me he might do that and not to be alarmed. I was not alarmed, but I cried even harder thinking about him taking his last breath during his death in my arms.

When my family arrived at the hospital, they led us to the chapel for family prayer. The nurses needed to do some post-death stuff to JJ and remove the final tubes that lingered in his body. They told us once he was all cleaned up they would come and get us so we could visit with him. The hospital staff was overly accommodating and very supportive, from the medical staff to the janitorial staff. Several of his nurses and aides cried and wiped away tears when they learned of JJ's death. The hospital was his second home. We had developed some great relationships there in those two years, two months and twenty days of his life.

Finally, they came to let me know I could bring family up to the room to see JJ. By the time everything was ready, there were lots of family members already at the hospital.

Our immediate and extended family was so large on my mother and my father's side; they had to split us into groups to visit with JJ. I went up to see him with the first group, which consisted of my maternal grandmother and my siblings. We opened the door to enter his room and I immediately became upset. I walked over to JJ's crib and pulled the white sheet off his face. They had covered him up from head to toe and it was too much for me. After the first few groups visited, I was drained and emotionally exhausted.

We were allowed to visit with JJ's body for several hours, but the time had come for my goodbye. The funeral home needed to pick up his body. Instead of packing us both up to head home as we had done for over two years, I left the hospital alone. The car ride home was the longest car ride ever, even though it normally took less than fifteen minutes on any given day. The day JJ died was definitely not a normal day. We pulled into the driveway, I gathered my belongings and went straight to my room. I sat down on my bed and looked around at all the things JJ and I had amassed in the space of our little room. I lay across my bed and wept. Tears streamed down my face until I drifted off to sleep.

I awoke to the sound of people talking in other parts of the house. I walked out of my room to see where all the noise was coming from. The living area was filled with lots of family and friends there to pay their respect. I received lots of hugs and condolences for my loss. I was handling my grief okay until I heard something that broke me down and sent me running to my room. Mom followed and asked what the problem was and if there was anything she could do to help. My nerves were shot. I could not handle the sound of a baby crying. I asked her if she would send anyone with a baby home because hearing another baby placed me in a bad spot emotionally.

I had to visit the funeral home to make preparations for JJ's services. It was so intense picking out a casket for a baby. I had never seen or heard of anything like that. The director was helpful and allowed me to take my time. I was in no rush to leave the place that held my son's body. I chose a beautiful baby blue casket, our favorite color, a headstone, burial plot, programs and decided to do a wake at the funeral home with the actual funeral service at my dad's church.

My dad was voted in as the new senior pastor of our original home church and ironically, JJ's funeral would be the first under his leadership. JJ was laid to rest there on a Saturday. One of my favorite aunts, Aunt Elyne blessed me by taking me to Sanger Harris, an upscale department store and allowed me to pick out anything I wanted to bury JJ in. I chose the cutest little three piece short set in his favorite color, baby blue, a cross necklace and a little blue and white stuffed puppy to lay with him in his casket.

The service was nice and the church was packed with family, friends and our new church family. My dad was prepared to do the eulogy, however I felt he would be too emotional so I asked a preacher friend of my parents, one of my ministry uncles I had grown to love, Uncle Ron. He did a great job. I looked out the window of the white limousine I rode in with my parents and siblings. JJ had the longest funeral procession I had ever seen. My son was buried at Restland Cemetery in Richardson, Texas, in a special section called Baby Land.

After the funeral and burial, I had to make some decisions regarding my life. I was still very distraught. I felt like I was too emotional to do well in college and decided not to go. Life was strange not having JJ around. I managed to get through the weeks one day at a time. I was mad at God for a long time. I wondered why He gave me this little boy only to take him from me. I had done the best job ever taking care of him...at least I thought I had for my age.

There came a time when God spoke to me in a way I finally understood. God let me know He chose me to endure this journey because He knew the strength He had given me. Although the beginning was not pleasant, He let me know the decisions we make in life can lead in one or two directions. Being in the projects of West Dallas that day was not a direction I chose and the end result was nothing I would have ever wished on any girl my age. My emotional breakdown as a result of that tragic event was a direction I could have changed. Looking back, I wish I had told my parents or an adult I trusted about what happened to me. If I had spoken up, maybe it could have changed JJ's life. I don't know. What I do know is God confirmed JJ's birth and the direction my life took was my destiny for the future and a message to be shared with others. I realized before my nineteenth birthday that I was chosen by God to carry this precious baby boy. I was chosen to make decisions for his life from the day he was conceived to the day he was born to the day he passed away. I was chosen to share my story with young girls and women who have encountered difficult situations regarding sexual assault or rape. I was chosen to remind them we all have a voice and it is never too late to speak out. I am Speaking UP Now for all of us who walked a similar journey, for only God knows the plans He has for OUR lives.

Innocence ***BEFORE*** Deception

By: Valarie D Gray

(Formerly Thompson, the Daughter of a Pastor)

Jaretton Jamal Thompson aka JJ was born June 10, 1982. He passed away on August 20, 1984, at the precious age of two. JJ, whom many had grown to love, was survived by his teenage mother, a large family, a circle of friends and medical staff from Children's Medical Center of Dallas. This little boy, along with his mother's faith and determination, impacted many lives.

The doctors predicted JJ would live approximately six months in his terminally ill condition; however, he beat their odds. The love God placed in his mother's heart allowed JJ to be cared for in a loving home for two years, two months and twenty days despite his severe birth defects.

JJ's mom believes what God allowed to happen in her life helped to make her a strong individual. She considers herself a true testament of faith. Valarie desires to be an example to others facing life challenges that may be too unbelievable to imagine. Her naïvety and innocence made her the vulnerable target of bullying. Placing her trust in another person, she was manipulated and led through a series of circumstances culminating in traumatic assault. From experiencing an unwanted pregnancy to making the decision to care for a terminally ill child at the young age of fifteen, these events helped manifest her into the woman she is today and to God she is grateful.

Valarie Gray

14

Pictures of *Love*...Beginning to End,

Jaretton Jamal Thompson

- Fifteen, pregnant and sad
- JJ "outgrowing" the loaner incubator from the Children's Medical Center of Dallas
- JJ get's a break from his warmer
- The big boy JJ taking a nap after drinking from a bottle
- Mommy talking to JJ asking, why the sad face
- A delicious "special formula" delivered through his tube
- Check out that "sleep" grin from JJ bundled up for body temperature control
- A miracle 1st birthday celebration (post hospital stay)
- JJ loving on Mommy after Easter service
- My mommy "purposely" said BOO to scare me
- Wired up at his second home
- I absolutely lived at Children's Medical Center anytime JJ was hospitalized
- Our only studio picture

Fifteen, Pregnant and sad

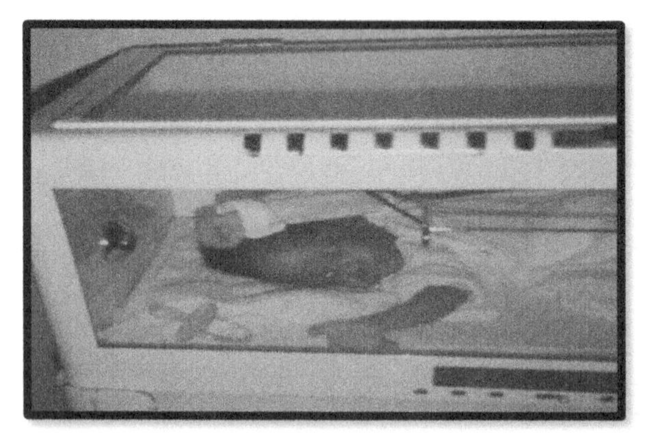

JJ "outgrowing" the loaner incubator from the Children's Medical Center of Dallas

JJ gets a break from his warmer

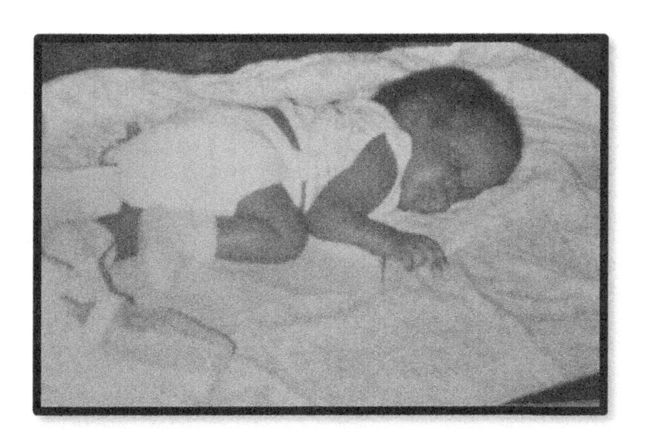

The big boy JJ taking a nap after drinking from a bottle

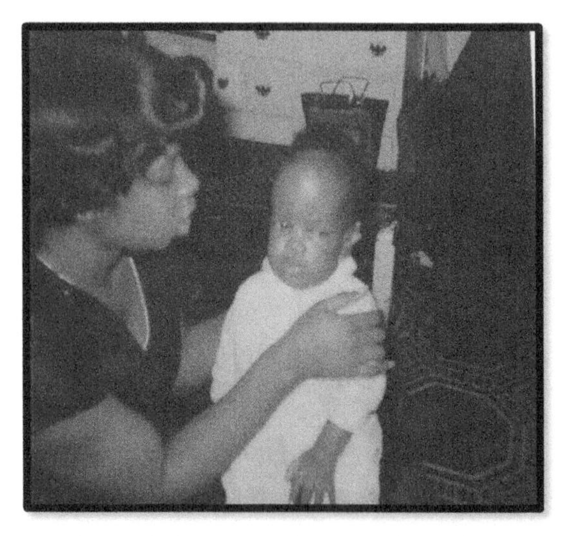

Mommy talking to JJ asking, why the sad face

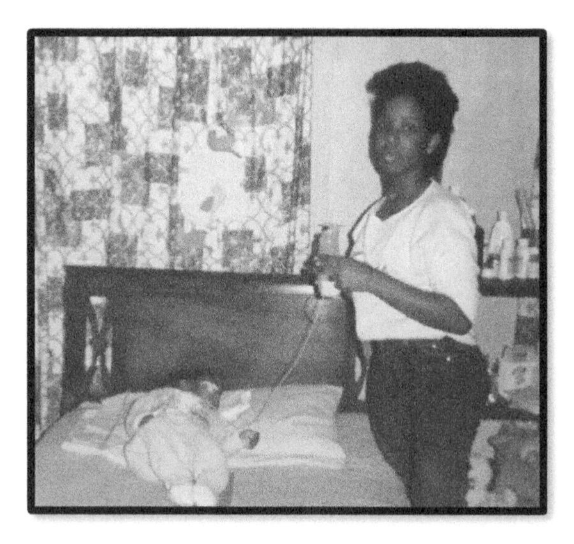

A delicious "special formula" delivered through his tube

Check out that "sleep" grin from JJ bundled up for body temperature control

A miracle 1st birthday celebration (post hospital stay)

JJ loving on Mommy after Easter service

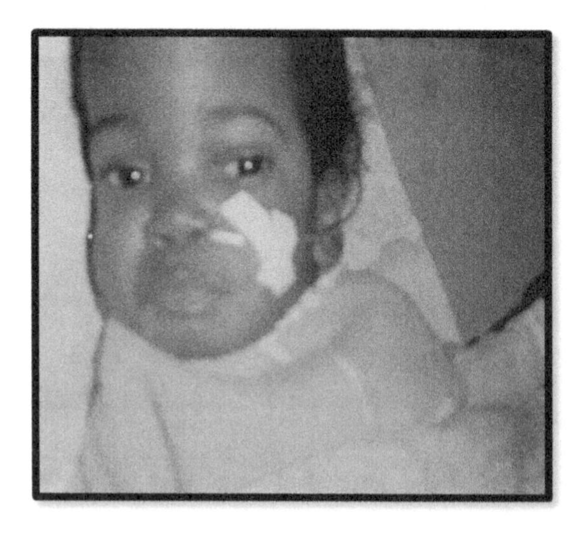

My Mommy "purposely" said BOO to scare me

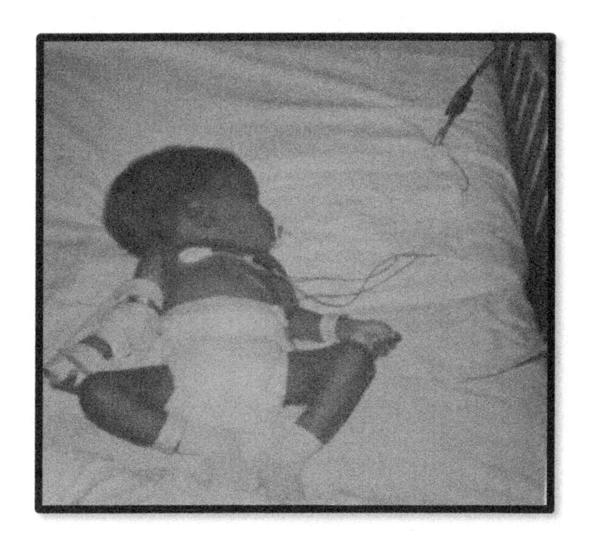

Wired up at his second home

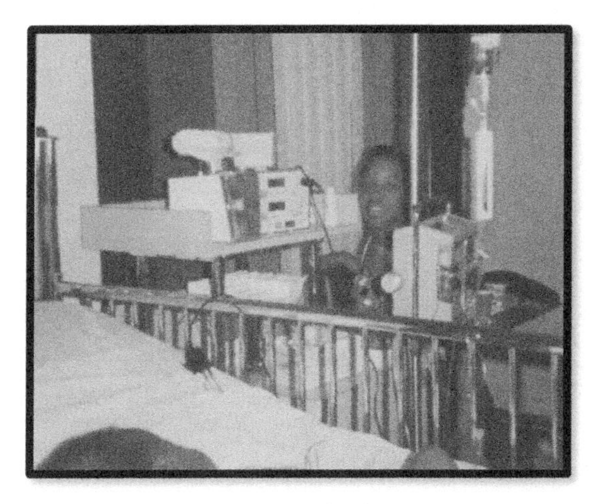

I absolutely lived at Children's Medical Center anytime JJ was hospitalized

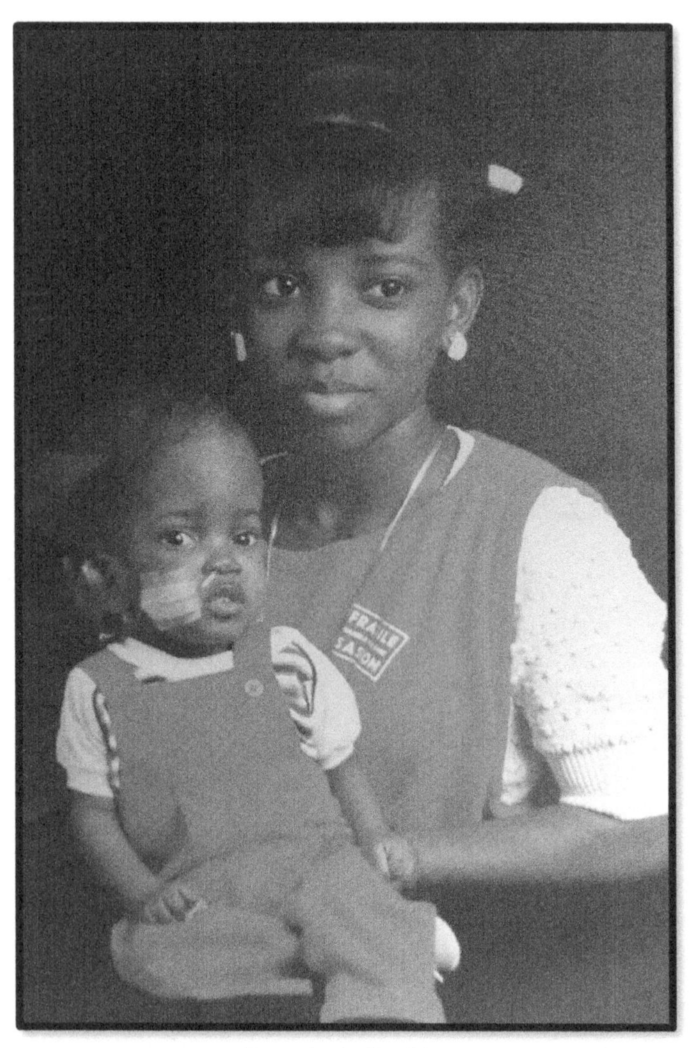

Our only studio picture

Made in the USA
Monee, IL
08 July 2023

38571966R00079